The Bard in Love

Joy Sengupta is an Indian film and stage actor who has worked extensively in Bollywood cinema, Bengali cinema as well as theatre. He is trained in theatre studies, specializing in acting, under the legendary Ebrahim Alkazi at Living Theatre Academy. He is best known for his debut feature, *Hazaar Chaurasi Ki Maa* (1998) directed by the celebrated Govind Nihalani. Joy has acted in over 16 films in Hindi, 18 films in Bengali, and 3 films in English (including an US-UK co-production on the Bhopal Gas Tragedy). Ten of those have received international awards. He has worked as an actor in five web series (including a European series) and 25 telefilms and over 50 ad commercials, along with five radio dramas for *BBC Radio 4*, including Vikram Seth's *A Suitable Boy* and Shakespeare's *The Two Gentlemen of Verona*. He is also known for dubbing for Chris Evans as Steve Rogers/Captain America in Marvel Cinematic Universe films in Hindi.

Joy has worked with legendary directors like Habib Tanveer, Safdar Hashmi, M.K. Raina, Barry John, Lillete Dubey, and Feroz Khan. He has also performed globally in West End (London), Off Broadway (New York), Edinburgh Festival Fringe, etc.

Joy was presented the V. Shantaram award for acting in his debut film *Hazaar Chaurasi Ki Maa*. He was awarded the Mahindra Excellence in Theatre Award for the year 2006, for portraying M.K. Gandhi in the play *Sammy*.

Joy has donned many caps throughout his journey in the cultural spheres. He was a teacher of theatre in schools across Delhi. He has taught creative communication at management schools. In his own unique style, he has used theatre as a tool for literacy, for Literacy Mission. He conducts regular sessions on theatre and cinema appreciation.

Prasun Roy is a bestselling author known for his accessible narrative style across genres including biography, horror, crime thrillers, mythology, history, and the paranormal. A researcher of India's unsung freedom fighters, his acclaimed work on Rash Behari Bose highlights significant INA contributions towards India's freedom struggle. Two of his fiction titles for young adults have been selected as supplementary reads for students at a prominent school in Vadodara. A few of his works with eminent publishers have been taken up for audio-video (AV) adaptations too. He has also translated classics by Rabindranath Tagore and Bibhutibhushan Bandyopadhyay for global readers.

A heritage enthusiast, Prasun serves as convenor of Indian History Awareness and Research (IHAR) and is a life member of Indian National Trust for Art and Cultural Heritage (INTACH). He has been a prominent speaker at many prestigious literary festivals, including Tata Steel Kolkata Literary Meet, Apeejay Kolkata Literary Festival and Pune International Literary Festival, among others.

An alumnus of IIM Lucknow, he lives in Kolkata and manages his family's pharmaceutical business headquartered in Vadodara and Kolkata.

The Bard in Love

Tagore and His Timeless Ladies

PRASUN ROY
and JOY SENGUPTA

RUPA

Published by
Rupa Publications India Pvt. Ltd 2026
161-B/4, Gulmohar House,
Yusuf Sarai Community Centre,
New Delhi 110049

Sales centres
Bengaluru Chennai
Hyderabad Kolkata Mumbai

The views and opinions expressed in this book are the authors' own and the facts are as reported by them; these have been verified to the extent possible, and the publishers are not in any way liable for the same.

P-ISBN: 978-93-5352-883-6
E-ISBN: 978-93-5352-218-6

First impression 2026

10 9 8 7 6 5 4 3 2 1

Printed in India

Contents

Sonar Tori
The Golden Boat

Prologue

To
Rabindranath Tagore

Welcome, my dear friend. I welcome you into this world and into this life!

The journey ahead is long, tiring, yet exciting—it is a journey where you and I shall together discover some wonders. As your pal, I would love to scream out to the entire world the fantastic tale of this voyage. I know it might make you feel sad, confused or even angry. However, we both shall know that it is something that you and I have experienced together. Remember, my dear, you shall be my 'best friend' forever. Thus, I can gather the courage to whisper out this weird tale of a life that we shall live together as inseparable entities.

You might be sceptical whether everything needs to be said or not, but trust me, the two of us need to know about them. Love is the purest of all emotions, so let us feel that gift from the universe. Life is too short to wait in contemplation.

My friend, there is no parameter in this world that clearly demarcates the distinction between right and wrong. No scale can judge between virtues and vice. So, let us be fearless, my friend; the world is not perfect enough to judge the vibes of the human heart.

Yet, remember, it is but our blessing and our curse that both of us would remain each other's confidante forever! We might struggle to detach ourselves, but destiny would never let it happen. We might be companionless for our entire lives, but we shall always be united in our hearts.

Dear Rabindranath, as the new dawn begins, let me embrace you and whisper into your ears that I am now revealing the tale of my 'best friend' in front of the entire human race.

Yours truly,
Robi, your 'inner soul'

Jorashako
The Beginning

Usha—A New Dawn

'Every child comes with the message that God is not yet discouraged of man…'

July 1868.
Tagore Mansion. Jorashako, Bengal.

The month of July in 1868 had a special place in the heart of destiny that sketched a unique picture in the future of the stalwart Tagore family. Amid the humid climate, flutes of festivity played the sweet music to usher in an enigma within the sprawling mansion of the Tagore family in Jorashako. It was Maharshi Debendranath Tagore's fifth son Jyotirindranath's wedding.

The tall pillars and walls received their ample dose of whitewash, while the aged glass chandelier got rid of its mesh of cobweb and dust and became decorated with candles, whose flickering flames sparkled like gemstones. Shimmery curtains flowed down from the roofs and announced the commencement of the ceremony. Even the neglected 'Golabari' (the deserted barn house that was no longer used for the purpose it was built) got scrubbed and washed. The damp air carried the fragrance of attar and lent an intoxicating aroma around the Tagore Mansion.

Through the canopy of protection, under the strict supervision of an able servant, the little rebellious boy stood beside a tall door at the end of the huge corridor and peeped. He was eight years old, but he was like a tempest. The youngest child in the huge family was just as overlooked as the decade-old terracotta flower vase sitting lonely upon the mahogany table.

'Brajeswar, is she the new bride of Jyotidada? She looks so young and little!' questioned the boy.

The dark skinned, big-eyed, long-haired but stout head-servants replied, 'Yes, Robi baba. She is the one...'

With his large expressive eyes, he witnessed the panorama as a little girl dressed in a traditional wedding saree walked upon the marble floor with her soft and naive footsteps. The slender gold bracelets tinkled upon her delicate brown arms, while the gaudy necklace perhaps made her a bit uncomfortable, as she shyly tried to hide her face behind the half-drawn veil.

Maybe she noticed the little boy standing afar, or maybe she didn't; nobody knew. For a moment, she halted and lifted her eyes from behind her veil. Immediately, the ladies of the house surrounded her like a swarm of bees and took her inside the inner apartments that were solely designated for the women of the family.

A sparkle glittered in the eyes of the little boy as he exclaimed in excitement, '*Bouthakrun*!'

Three months ago—
Jorashako, Bengal.
1868.

Rabindranath Tagore, aka *Robi*, was the youngest scion of the family. The grandeur of the Tagore Mansion, along with the fortunes of the Tagore family, had seen a sudden trough ever since the death of his grandfather, Prince Dwarkanath Tagore. Yet, the aristocracy of the family survived all odds to retain its magnificence while Debendranath, along with his elder sons, laboured to bring back the prosperity.

On a usual routine day, existence had a subtle loneliness in the life of little Robi. A loneliness that was never voiced in words or expressed in cravings. Confined within the massive ancestral mansion, the tempest within him brewed up and desperately sought an outburst. That day, too, was no exception...

'Wake up, it's morning.' The voice of Brajeswar reverberated around the corners of his ears and plucked away the blanket of sleep from his body. Robi woke up with a startle and looked at the window. The sun was still reluctantly below the horizon, and a few stray rays were faintly trying to peep in. With a splash of cold water over his face, Robi rubbed off the remaining specks of sleep and headed out for the first activity in his daily routine.

In the specially prepared flat ground (created by digging and loosening the soil and pouring an extravagance of mustard oil) stood the famous one-eyed wrestler, *Kana Pehlwan*, ready for his pupil.

'Let us begin...' growled the man while Robi charged ahead for his heartily unwanted lesson of wrestling. For the trainer, the stalwart wrestler, it was child's play to pin down his heavily unmatched pupil upon the ground and smear his entire body with an overload of dust and dirt.

As Robi struggled to overcome his *Guru,* his sleep-ridden heart felt no intention to defeat him. Finally, after every bit of languor vanished from his eyes and every muscle of his body became active, Robi went inside to cleanse himself. Yet, it was just the beginning of the day! As soon as he came out, he saw the student from the Medical College standing at the veranda with a wide grin. Noticing the glistering array of his teeth, which seemed to reflect the incoming sunlight, Robi wondered what foray of speech was waiting behind them to be showered upon him.

The next hour went like a brief whirlwind as Robi sat in front of the spooky skeleton, hanging from the wall of his bedroom, as his avid teacher dictated to him the names of bones in the weird session on Osteology.

The skeleton, however, was the subject of his wild deliberation as the little boy sat blankly with a purely attentive countenance. Within his mind, Robi asked himself, '*I wonder what the owner of the skeleton looked like? How was his life? Was it funny, was it sad, was it adventurous? Was he a wicked man or a holy man? Was he ordinary to look at, or was he handsome?*'

Robi chuckled within his mind as another question flashed up: '*Was it a man or a woman? This skeleton hangs in front of our eyes perpetually, yet we know so little about it...*'

Then, as a cool breeze gushed in through the window and fluttered his hair carelessly, an even more gripping idea choked his throat: '*What if...the apparition of the skeleton's true owner comes and visits me in the middle of the night? I am fiddling with the final remains of his or her mortal existence. What if he or she gets really angry with me and wakes me up on a moonless night?'*

As a lump appeared in his throat, Robi gulped down his own saliva and tried to forget the scary thoughts. Thankfully, the class ended soon and gave respite to his frightened soul.

At seven o'clock, Master Nilkamal arrived, and Robi sat with him for his regular dose of Bengali, Arithmetic, Algebra, Geometry, and almost every possible subject that could be taught to a pupil in that era. The overdose of education was showered like an array of arrows while Robi adapted himself into a perforated sheet that let each of them pass through unhindered without being stuck onto him.

Sitting with his chalk and slate, his mind floated towards the old tailor with thick-glassed spectacles who sat on the veranda. He wondered, '*Only if I could earn the limitless freedom that this man enjoys as he sits and sulks in the sunlight for hours!*'

At nine o'clock, Govinda, the second-in-command of the staff of servants, came with a dirty yellow towel to take him for his bath. Fifteen minutes later arrived the routine meal of rice, pulses and fish curry. The meticulously chosen meal was meant to keep his gastronomical juices under control while he struggled to hold his attention at school from ten to four in the afternoon.

After returning from school, Robi got a little bout of snack before he throttled himself into a rigorous tenure of exercise session followed by a creative hour of drawing class. Evening came unnoticed, like every day, as Robi craved to get a glimpse of the colourful dusk with her crimson rays. Then, as the veil of the evening settled upon the infinite sky, it was time for him to sit with Master Aghor, who arrived with his overflowing potion of English lessons.

Finally, as the day came to an end, Robi was fully exhausted, both physically and mentally. Signing off with dinner, he got tucked into bed, inside his mother's room, for a supposed good night's sleep.

Tucked in under the sheets, as his eyelids became heavy, Robi felt happy and sighed, '*At last, in my dreams, I can become a free bird!*'

Luckily, the next morning was Sunday. It was the only day of the week when the grinding mill of the routine allowed Robi a respite from the mechanical drill.

Monsoon was his favourite. Being the month of April, the monsoon had just made her much-coveted entry. It gave him a sense of boundless ecstasy, and his heart jumped crazily within his ribcage. Peeping through the large Venetian shutters of the sprawling veranda, Robi stared at the raindrops rushing down from the clouds and crashing upon the thirsty bosom of Mother Earth. In the absence of company, the public pool at a distance from the Tagore Mansion was a spot where his eyes lurked through the Venetian shutters for a glimpse of different human characters.

Sunday mornings were his favourite. Yet, this Sunday was even more special. The gathering of dark clouds across the morning sky, the chill in the air and the supple fragrance of the soil had an intoxicating madness. Robi finished his breakfast and arrived at his favourite corner in the veranda. He extended his hands through the iron railings and felt the droplets of rain. The drizzle had not yet gained momentum. Robi carefully collected a few drops on his palm and then drank them with a refreshing sip.

Then, he took out his toy cane and stood in front of the array of railings. In his loneliness, he had invented a wonderful game! It was his classroom, and they were his disobedient students, who didn't even care to answer him!

Robi lashed his cane upon the prodigal students and commanded, 'You naughty, disobedient folks, with this level of merit you have no hope of a good future! I am sure, when you grow up you would be fit for nothing but casual labour!'

As the hour proceeded and the drizzle gained pace, Robi went inside for his next escapade. The Durga Puja festivities were still afar. However, amid the overdose of stories from Brajeswar, he had heard many stories of animal sacrifices. The wooden lion stood at a corner of a neglected room, and Robi pondered, '*Being a budding Zamindar, I must introduce my valiance with a lion sacrifice!*'

Thus, with a frail wooden stick, he thrusted lethal blows upon the innocent wooden lion and relished a heavenly ecstasy, while the monsoon showers accompanied him with their incessant applause. Robi appended the ritual with his creative *mantra*...

Liony, liony, off with your head,
Liony, liony, now you are dead.
Woofle the walnut goes clappety clap,
Snip, snop, SNAP!

As lunch time got over, the rains receded a bit, and Robi found himself all by his own, while the women and the men rested in their respective quarters. He snuck out into the courtyard and hid himself inside the belly of the long-unused palanquin (lying idly within the courtyard). This was his favourite haunt to sit and daydream. In his dreams, his imaginary buddies kept him company. Hidden away from the eyes of the household, it was a world of his own that followed his own rules.

That afternoon, Robi felt melancholic. It was a sadness that he couldn't understand. Perhaps it was the absence of a companion that depressed him. He closed his eyes and said to himself, '*I wish I could have a friend. A person who would be just like me and would play with me...*' Something came to his mind, and he rushed out. Then, he ran towards the solitary *Golabari* (barn house). Beside it stood a Peepal tree. Robi remembered that Brajeswar had once told him that on its topmost branch, it hosted a *Brahmodaittyo*, a *Brahmin* ghost, who had magical powers. The Peepal was supposed to be a wishing tree, even though nobody ever considered it so!

In a whimsical fancy, Robi tore a piece of cloth, held it close to his heart and made a wish. Then, quietly, he tied it upon a branch of the tree. The soil was still wet and muddy. The remnant raindrops still dripped from the leaves. Robi hid the branch among other branches and ran back. He had heard that if anyone tied a piece of cloth ingrained with a wish, upon a wishing tree, if that wish was granted, then the knot automatically opened and the cloth vanished!

A big droplet trickled from the topmost leaf, made its way through the foliage and fell on the piece of cloth. Maybe the Brahmodaittyo showered a silent acknowledgement for the innocent wish.

A Week after the Wedding—
Tagore Mansion. Jorashako, Bengal.
July 1868.

In the boredom of the afternoon, Robi sat inside the Golabari and wondered about the first glimpse of the new bride of Jyotidada. Even through her veiled countenance and ornamented attire, something told him that she was just like him. Within his mind, he contemplated, '*Did the Brahmodaittyo indeed hear my wish? Did Bouthakrun notice me? I really want to be friends with her...*'

The festivities of the wedding had culminated, and soon everything had melted into the normal routine. However, the new bride was fortified within the inner chambers of the ladies. To be more precise, she was assigned the room adjoining the roof of the inner suites.

Little Robi was desperate to find out the truth. Hence, he tried every possible method to make an acquaintance. Despite his heavily crunched-up schedule, he managed to churn out precious minutes to go around and seek an opportunity to talk to her. Then again, a question clouded his imagination: '*What will I ask her when I meet her? I don't have any reason to talk to her. I just want to know if she is the friend whom Brahmodaittyo had granted for me. But I can't tell her so. What will she think?*'

Thus, from inside the partition created by an invisible sheet, he witnessed the little girl get the attention of the women of the family, while he stared at her blatantly through an equally invisible perforation in that sheet.

One evening, Robi saw the new bride walking on the roof with his elder sister. The two of them were giggling and chatting while they strolled on the roof. Robi stood near the adjacent staircase and watched. It was the first time that he saw her full face. It was the innocent face of a little girl whose countenance still held a childish unsophistication. Her large eyes, her dusky complexion and her lucid behaviour combined to reveal an enigma.

In his young heart, Robi felt happy. Her smile made him smile, even though he was standing at a distance and away from her sight. Mesmerized by the moment, Robi walked up to the rooftop, almost involuntarily. Then, an unexpected stumble upon the threshold of the stairs brought him back to consciousness.

'*Oh! I have come outside the boundaries laid down for the boys!*' he exclaimed within his own mind. An unknown shudder curtailed his onward stance, and Robi headed back towards his own room. He was visibly disappointed as a golden opportunity to familiarize with the new member of the family was just marred.

Yet, his subconscious mind told him, '*She looks mischievous. However, being the new bride, she can't indulge in her mischievousness. One day, I will surely find out. She is unique... I can feel it.*'

During his return journey, Robi took a reroute and went beside the Golabari. He approached the Peepal tree and then pulled the branches. As he searched, his heart again began to palpitate excitedly. The piece of cloth that he had tied was gone!

With an ecstatic energy, he turned his eyes towards the window of the room on the roof. The faint figure of the new bride, the mysterious girl, was visible. Robi pondered, '*The cloth has vanished! I knew it. My wish has indeed come true. But did she just see what I was doing here? Did she get a hint of it?*'

The thoughts lingered inside his mind as he walked back. However, soon, with the grinding of his daily routine, it evaporated like camphor.

The following Sunday arrived with a secret plan. It was a plan about which Robi was completely oblivious. Like every Sunday, he had planned his daily exploits. However, his weeklong failed attempts to make friends with the new bride made him feel somewhat dejected. Yet, he finished his breakfast and went over to the array of railings.

It was time for him to conduct his rigorous classroom sessions where he was the teacher and his disobedient students were once again ready to exhibit their defiance. Robi took his toy cane and stood in front of the rails. Without any dialogue, he whipped them angrily and then stood with a fuming expression!

'Why don't you ever learn?' he exclaimed. 'Your disobedience and lack of interest in education are making me furious! I will punish you so much that you will never be able to talk! Well, you don't talk otherwise, but this will make you speechless forever...'

Hehehe, a giggle reverberated. It was an unfamiliar voice. Nonetheless, it was a sweet and fluty feminine voice that echoed momentarily and stopped.

A sudden shock gripped Robi. It was a blend of surprise and fear, and he quickly turned around. Then, he froze like a piece of stone! In a state of spellbound amazement, he saw that his new Bouthakrun was standing behind him.

The little girl came ahead cautiously and said softly, 'Would you be a guest? There is a wedding in my doll's house!'

Robi fumbled. He didn't know what to say. The new bride had just seen his whimsical secret game, and he felt totally embarrassed. Still unable to recover completely, he said in a muffled tone, 'I...actually mean... What did you say?'

The little girl was dressed in a simple cotton *saree* and stood in front of him. From her face, it was clear that she was suppressing a hearty laughter. She looked into his eyes and said, 'I am Kadambari. I am the new bride of your Jyotidada.'

'I will call you Bouthakrun!' blurted Robi with excitement. He felt ecstatic. He added, 'Will you be my friend? Everyone in this house is older than me. I don't have anyone to play with or to chat with. Will you be my...'

'Yes...' Kadambari replied with an innocently shy expression. Then she continued, 'In my room on the roof, there is a wedding at the doll's house in the afternoon. I have come here to invite you as the chief guest!'

'Oh wow!' replied Robi and stood quiet. His mind flew to many questions about what the elders would say.

Kadambari replied, 'Maa and your sister would be so happy! I told them that you would surely agree.'

Hence, that evening, Robi got dressed in his best and reached the mysterious doorway to the room of his new pal, his Bouthakrun. Within the room, the doll's house had received a fantastic decoration. Adorned with flowers and pieces of colourful paper, the toy bride and groom sat outside the house. Robi's sister was sitting upon the bedstead while Kadambari made arrangements for her coveted guest.

Robi felt special as the guest of honour. Upon the floor were spread out the banana-leaf plates. He received a grand welcome and was asked to take his seat on the floor for the feast to begin.

Kadambari, dressed in a pretty silk *saree*, knelt and placed four pieces of sweetmeat on the leaf plate. Robi picked up one piece and took a bite.

'How is it?' chuckled Kadambari with excitement.

The delicacy melted within his mouth and dissolved his heart. Almost instantaneously, he closed his eyes and said with a smile, 'Bouthakrun, it is heavenly...'

Laughter and giggles combined to create the foundation of a beautiful and innocent relationship. Robi and Kadambari became best pals that evening. Yet, destiny knew that it was the first step that their souls took towards an unblemished relationship, which was to become an integral part of Robi's and Kadambari's existence!

Life was simple, and the purity of their childhood melded effortlessly. Perhaps, the invisible Brahmodaittyo smiled happily from the topmost branch of the Peepal tree.

Ribhu—The Hearts Evolve

'Real friendship is like fluorescence; it shines better when everything has darkened...'

That evening, before leaving, Robi whispered into Kadambari's ear, 'This mansion has many wonders. I will show them to you. Don't tell anyone, it will be our secret adventure...'

'When?' Kadambari asked softly. Her eyes reflected a playful curiosity, hidden behind a thin sheath of inhibition.

'Soon, Bouthakrun... Very soon!' replied Robi as he hurried away to avoid a scrutinizing glance from his sister.

Then, the days moved and the nights passed...

The grinding routine of Robi hardly spared him any respite during the weekdays. Yet, the dormant spirit within the mischievous boy had found his angel amid that ocean of monotony. Nothing could keep him bound.

Chandimandap, the outer veranda where the school was held, was his strict destination to sit and consume the overflow of knowledge. It was a place where Robi often felt the stabs of drowsiness. However, something metamorphosed after one morning, a few days later.

It was a humid morning, and the air carried a secret message about an upcoming tempest.

Robi lifted his eyes from his slate, where he was scribbling his classwork, and looked up. His glance meandered towards the parapet-surrounded roof of the inner apartment, and his glimpse froze! Kadambari was roaming about playfully. A manservant was carefully keeping some flowerpots along the parapet, while Kadambari was showering down her meticulous instructions about their proper placement.

For a moment, her eyes turned down and met his eyes. A smile got painted on both their countenances, and Robi felt happy. He knew, every day, his pal, his Bouthakrun, would come across that parapet to water the blooms. A glimpse of her appearance, carelessly wandering with her doll in her hands, evoked a sense of freedom in Robi. He knew her occasional glimpses through the purple petals of the bougainvillaea would give him the joy to finish his work and then steal away some precious moments to meet her.

His heart leapt inside his ribcage. '*Bouthakrun is new in the Tagore Mansion, and I must show her everything that I can. None of the others can witness those glorious visions amid the mundane walls of this mansion! She is like the new tourist, while I am an ardent guide…*'

That evening, the tempest did brew up and brought in the dark clouds. Robi's routine received a little imbalance, and he ran across the inner apartments and reached the room on the roof. Kadambari was sitting inside her room, deeply absorbed in the pages of a book. As per norm, Jyotidada was not at home; he was busy with his colossal amount of work, somewhere.

'Quick, Bouthakrun! Come with me!' blurted little Robi. It was the spirited summons of a newfound friend to another to explore the unexplored territory of fun.

He held her hand and dragged her along, while she ran to keep pace and tried to gauge the sudden surprise. As they reached the ground floor, Robi hurried towards the western boundary. The sky was shrouded by the rainclouds that curtained the sunlight and obscured visibility. The larger droplets of rain summoned the commencement of the downpours. In harmony, the aroma of the wet soil filled the air.

'Look,' whispered Robi, 'do you see that ghastly creature? I knew, during such a tumultuous moment, I would be able to spot that apparition!'

Kadambari's glance followed his fingers and tried to see. Amid that stormy chaos, the *Badaam* tree, on the western corner of the mansion, swayed gently in the breeze.

'Did you see that mysterious shape with one foot on the tree and the other on the third-floor cornice?' asked Robi excitedly.

Indeed, in that kaleidoscope of fading sunlight and consuming darkness, something appeared as the swaying legs of a ghastly phantom from folklore.

Then, as a dash of lightning flashed across the sky and illuminated everything, Kadambari laughed loudly and said, 'Robi, that is just the tree and its leaves! There are no ghosts in this house! Don't tell me that you are scared of such a thing?'

A pang of embarrassment flushed across his face, but he defended his demeanour with, 'Wait, I will show you what I meant...'

He took Kadambari and hurried towards the solitary Golabari. Beside it stood the Peepal tree. The downpour had begun incessantly, and the two went out in the open. The endless drops of rain drenched them and the Peepal tree.

Robi stood and said excitedly, 'That Peepal tree hosts a Brahmodaittyo on its topmost branch. That creature has magical powers! We just saw a glimpse of his frame at the western corner. It was not an illusion; it was HIM. I know it. With his powers, this tree has become a wishing tree! Days ago, I had tied a piece of cloth on one of the branches with a wish…a wish for a friend! Now see, on the day you arrived, that knot vanished and…'

Robi paused a bit, took a deep breath and added, 'Bouthakrun…my wish got granted!'

Kadambari smiled happily, while a few elusive teardrops got hidden amid the pouring showers. She replied, 'Yes, Robi. I believe you because you are my friend. Yes, I trust that the myth is true!'

As Robi tried to smile back, Kadambari started to spin around him in a euphoric dance and laughed heartily, 'But I just discovered another huge truth. Robi Babu is scared of ghosts! Hahaha…'

Robi felt cross, as his momentary self-actualization got shattered, and he darted indoors angrily while Kadambari swirled around in that incessant downpour to soak herself in that untamed freedom! Even amid that fleeting anger and embarrassment, the sweet bond of friendship deepened between the two. Through that innocent attachment, Robi gained unhindered access to the inner quarters, especially in the company of his little Bouthakrun!

A few days passed, or even a week, or maybe a fraction of a fortnight. Then, a prized Sunday morning arrived…

Robi tiptoed to his new buddy and told her, 'Today, I shall show you some wonders that I have secretly discovered to enjoy the monotony of this huge palatial mansion.'

He was excited to pour out his heart to his new pal. In her eyes, he witnessed the mischievous rebel that he had harnessed within his own heart.

The new bride, yet a little girl, was still adjusting to the norms of the colossal Tagore family. It was a mammoth duty amid that sombrely conservative household. The moments of unblemished companionship with Robi, the only person of comparable age, defined her escapade into the pasture of her own childhood. Robi's little world created an energetic enthusiasm within her.

Sunday mornings were usually busy in that enormous joint-family and the two waited patiently for noon. As midday arrived, the family members, as well as the entourage of servants, went inside their own lazy, leisurely abodes. Robi and Kadambari arrived upon the open, unfenced roof of the outer apartments. It was atop the strict male-dominated arena of the outer quarters. However, none of the men were around on a coveted holiday afternoon.

'I climb here secretly during midday,' said Robi. 'I just love this escapade.'

As Kadambari stood beside him, he continued, 'Look, the entire expanse beyond Chitpore Road, with the vast stretch of houses and open land, is visible from here! As far as the eye can see, you can perhaps witness the entire Calcutta from here! Isn't it beautiful? The enormity of the sky above, the empty Ghat over there, the innumerable colourful rooftops spread over the city… It is so beautiful. You can feel like a king or a queen of the gigantic city!'

Kadambari was speechless. She took a deep breath and seeped in the vibrant energy of the vastness. Then, she replied softly, 'Yes, the vastness is stunning…'

The ensuing silence got pierced by the shrill voice of a vendor on the street, '*I-i-i-ce Kulpi… Come* and take a cone of this cool and delicious Lolli to get respite from the heat!'

'Do you like *Kulpi* ice Lolli?' asked Robi. 'I often see this man vending his delicacies. Alas, being a kid, it's not the norm to get out alone and grab one. I secretly plan to grab one after I manage to earn a little pocket money for my virtuous behaviour. Would you like to have one too?'

In a big pot filled with lumps of ice, the man was carrying his treasure of tin containers full of the flavoursome delicacy. A glitter sparkled in Robi's eyes, and Kadambari smiled back at him. Perhaps she understood the loneliness that dwelt within him.

She nodded her head, but Robi could hardly comprehend whether it was a 'yes' or a 'no'.

He paused a while and then asked, 'Alright, we don't have enough time to waste. The tour must continue; else we won't be able to complete it… Now, would you like to board a magical vessel and hear the tales of Abdul the sailor?'

The outline of Dukhon, the water bearer, became visible at a distance. He was fetching water from the Ganges in his yoke to fill the brimming water pots of the Tagore Mansion. Kadambari felt a bit uneasy and replied, 'Yes, let us go from here...'

Thus, away from everyone's eyes, the two mismatched pals went into another adventure joyride, inside the damp belly of the long unused palanquin (lying idly within the courtyard). Then, the favourite haunt of solitary Robi transformed into his ship of dreams.

As they crouched inside the palanquin, Kadambari giggled in playful excitement, and Robi began his oration, 'This is not just an abandoned palanquin, as everyone thinks. It is a vessel of dreams that has so many tales within its aged body. As I float into a daze, this becomes my enchanted peacock-boat that takes me on a joyride. I prefer to imagine Abdul as the captain of that ship. He has credence!'

'Well, Abdul is not my imagination. Abdul the sailor was a valiant man...' he stated after a pause.

She replied in a low voice, 'Who is Abdul?'

'Abdul was a sailor. He used to bring *Hilsa* fish and turtle eggs from the Padma River for my elder brothers...' said Robi in a majestic voice that was full of excitement.

'Where is he now?' asked Kadambari inquisitively.

'One day, he went in search of news for me, along with more Hilsa and turtle eggs for the others, but he never returned...' sighed Robi.

'Oh my god. Did he die? What news did he go to fetch?' she asked.

'For that, you need to know the whole story!' he replied with an impish smile. 'But I am sure he is alive. I think he is like a cockroach that can manage to stay alive at any cost.'

'Now, close your eyes while I tell you his fantastic saga...' added Robi, after a moment.

Kadambari closed her eyes while her eyelashes quivered with curiosity. Robi began his magnificent speech: 'Abdul had a distinct appearance. With his pointed beard, his shaven moustache and close-cropped head, he was a pious yet brave sailor. Let me tell you a tale of his bravery that is very dear to me...well, not because I had a significant contribution in refining the brilliance in it, but it is indeed a brilliant one.'

He continued with an animated voice, 'One day, Abdul had gone out in a dinghy across the Padma River to catch fish, when a fierce gale commenced. The angry typhoon sank the boat, but brave Abdul seized the tow-rope with his teeth and swam ashore along with it!'

'Wow! He must have had really strong teeth,' smirked Kadambari, with her eyes closed.

Robi continued with rejuvenated energy, ignoring the pun in her words, 'That was not the end. As he turned his head, Abdul saw that a fierce panther had also been washed ashore beside him! That wild animal was hungry and was about to pounce upon him with his sharp teeth and glaring eyes. Alas, the creature was unaware of Abdul's courage. He quickly made a noose with his tow rope and threw it across the panther's neck before it could leap! Whilst the animal struggled, the noose grew tighter and finally the panther gave in!'

'Did the panther die?' asked Kadambari.

'I had also asked the same question,' replied Robi seriously. 'No, it didn't. Abdul yoked the wild beast to his dinghy and made it tug him forty miles down the tumultuous river... So, a fifteen-hour journey was accomplished in two hours!'

Kadambari opened her eyes softly. Even though the credence of the tale was unexpectedly low, her heart had drifted into the turbulent Padma River to feel the adventure captured within it.

'The last day I met him,' added Robi, 'I asked him about more tales of the riverfront. He told me the story of the fearsome crocodile that had grabbed the billy goat of a gypsy woman from the shore and dragged it into the water. The infuriated gypsy woman jumped upon its back and began to sew her sickle at the throat of the beast! The furious and wounded crocodile plunged into the deeper waters and vanished along with the woman and the goat...'

'That is ghastly! What happened to the woman?' asked Kadambari as she sat within the old palanquin.

'I had asked that same question too...' replied Robi with a sigh. 'Alas, he went in search of that news for me, but he never returned.'

Kadambari felt sorry about the sorrowful climax of the story. But Robi reignited the energy and said confidently, 'Well, Abdul the brave is always going to be my sailor! I know he will come back soon...'

The relentless chatter of the little boy continued while the sparkle in the eyes of the young girl glittered like diamonds. Nonetheless, the midday floated into the afternoon and finally melted away towards the evening twilight. It was time to return to reality...but an unblemished bond had evolved in the young hearts.

The two of them snuck out from the palanquin and went indoors. As Kadambari stood near the staircase of the inner chambers of the ladies, she smiled back at her new friend and said, 'This was the best Sunday! I want to listen to more of your fantastic tales around the mansion.'

In the flickering light of the earthen lamp kept aside at a corner to illuminate the staircase, Robi exhibited a sardonic face and replied, 'Bouthakrun, those are my only stories! I don't have any more. In the absence of an ability to find or create more, I rewind within those same spheres again and again. I don't have any more tales that I can tell you...'

Kadambari patted him on his shoulder and said, 'Don't worry, I guess you will figure out how to be a good storyteller soon. Till then, I am glad that you are my playmate.'

'Goodnight,' responded Robi and then slowly vanished within the obscurity of the incoming evening. His heart whispered to his mind, 'This was the best Sunday ever...'

The tides of time moved ahead, and an innocent desire for companionship bloomed in both their hearts. Kadambari was ten years younger than her husband. In their marital relationship, Jyotirindranath became like her guardian and mentor. Jyotirindranath was a busy man, working for his literary endeavours as well as for the zamindari estate. However, within the little boy, Kadambari found a companion with whom she could play! Perhaps his company erased the vacuum in her life as she matured into a woman. It was the journey of growing up together, amid a conservative household that ignited an innocuous bond between the two! As the two grew up within the Tagore Mansion, Robi found an elation within her soul. In her eyes and her smile, he could discover self-respect.

Just as the bonds of friendship deepened, the relationship became even more mischievous. The two drew equal pleasures in creating some disruption that would harass the other and bring in a moment of respite, and that of pure fun. Yet, the absence of one another often made them sad.

Therefore, when Kadambari went to stay with her relatives, and a restless Robi couldn't find her slippers outside the door of her room, he would go into a frenzy and steal something valuable from her room to create a context for quarrel.

One evening, Kadambari returned home and began to search for her favourite gold-plated hairpin. The antique object was very dear to her, and she felt frustrated at not being able to locate it. Within her heart, she was sceptical about who might have hidden it.

Robi, who was loitering around her, commented playfully, 'Bouthakrun, do you expect me to keep an eye on your room when you go away? Am I a watchman?'

Kadambari replied crossly, 'You have no need to keep an eye on the room. Just keep a watch on your own hands!'

These bouts of deliberate quarrels were but expressions of a beautiful relationship.

Jyotirindranath became more and more busy, engaged mostly in the affairs of the Shelaidah estate or in his own theatrical and literary endeavours, which were gaining momentum and praise. Robi, his young brother, was his muse. Perhaps he understood the beauty of the relationship that Kadambari shared with him, or perhaps he didn't bother to delve into it. None knew. Despite so, whenever he was home, he enjoyed the company of the duo while he immersed himself in his soulful passions.

Kadambari converted the entire terrace into a wonderful garden, and Robi used to be enthralled by the beauty and colours of Mother Nature. Blossoms of *Chameli, Gandharaj, Rajnigandha, Karabi* and *Dolan-Champa* adorned the exquisite garden and made it look heavenly. Perhaps Robi's acumen for literature germinated somewhere within that colourful world.

Then, one day, Kadambari bought a Chinese *Shyama* bird and kept it as a pet. From under the covering of cloth placed over the cage in the veranda, the sweet whistling used to rise like a fountain. However, the chirping made Robi feel miserable.

He would hold his hands to his ears and wonder, '*The cries of that little bird are so heart-wrenching! I feel as if it is howling to be free and fly across the vast horizon!*'

As the daily supply of bird seed and insects, mostly grasshoppers, arrived from a hawker, Robi felt gruesomely unhappy.

Then, a few days later, Kadambari decided to keep pet squirrels in cages. At that point, the barrage of Robi's patience broke. He revolted, 'Bouthakrun, this is not right. This unnecessary caging of those poor creatures is a merciless act. Stop it!'

She sombrely replied with finesse, 'Do not make yourself my teacher! I know what I am doing.'

'Alright!' replied Robi angrily and went away.

That night, secretly, he released the bird and the squirrels. As they escaped from their confines, he laughed silently and danced along the staircase while he went back to his own room.

The next morning, Kadambari became furious, but she understood the craving for freedom within Robi's heart. A scuffle followed, but it was soaked in the sweet honey of friendship.

As the ripples of passing years took them beyond a decade-long existence, one evening, Robi sat beside Kadambari in a melancholic mood and said, 'Bouthakrun, I still don't have much to say. In this wide world, I don't have any stories. I have never excelled in anything in my life. Besides our daily quarrels or bouts of amusements, even to you, I don't have much to say! I really wish I could...'

She held his hand and replied, '*Ribhu*, or radiance, comes unnoticed to our lives; we don't need to worry. One day, you shall glisten too, like pure gold. The day will arrive when you will be able to discover that shine within you!'

To the entire household, Robi was a person who had no special importance. He was just as overlooked as the decade-old terracotta flower vase sitting lonely upon the mahogany table.

Yet, to her, he was special. It was a nameless love, never destined to be named.

**Bedroom of Debendranath Tagore. Tagore Mansion.
Jorashako, Bengal.
February 1873.**

'How would you like it if I take you to the Himalayas with me?' asked the sombre-voiced Debendranath with a calm demeanour.

The words floated inside the ears of Robi and created an avalanche of ecstasy from within his eardrums, passed through the neurons of his brain and then plunged into the cavity of his throbbing heart! His father had just offered him an opportunity to leave behind the confines of the Tagore Mansion and escape into the wild realms of the lofty Himalayas. This was too good to be true. It was an opportunity of a lifetime for a boy who had never seen the world beyond the high walls of the mansion.

Robi's heart wanted to say aloud, '*When the rains come down, I stretch out my hands through the iron railings of the veranda to feel the freedom encapsulated within those dews of heaven! My answer to your question... "How" ...would be a shriek of ecstasy that can shatter the skies!*'

In reality, he stood speechless and daydreamed with a smile pasted upon his lips.

'Hmmm...' rang the sombre voice, with the raise of an eyebrow. Debendranath was awaiting a response.

Robi jutted back from his dream and replied softly, with a bowed head, 'Yes, Baba, it would be an honour. I would love to go...'

As he walked down the stairs, after receiving a positive signal from his father, his mind again floated into a tidal wave of speculations. Soon after Robi's birth, his father had engaged himself in extensive travelling. Thus, Robi hardly got an opportunity to know his father. Whenever he returned, occasionally in between his tours, he came with foreign servants. In Robi's young heart, those new faces drew greater eagerness within him to make friends with them!

The immediate presence of Debendranath was a distant dream for Robi. Despite that, he never really felt a pang for that association. Perhaps the long spans of disassociation had created a gap. Often when Debendranath was home, Robi would hide around the staircase to the second floor during early dawn, and watch the man who was markedly his own glorious father. At a distance, the serene-bodied Debendranath sat on the roof, silent as an image of white marble, with his hands folded upon his lap, deeply engrossed in his morning prayers. It was only a sense of reverence that got ignited within the child, but the soul remained alien. The journey to the Himalayas was an opportunity to melt that icy wall in between, and Robi felt eager.

Yet, as he descended the steps, another thought blew in the sentiments of remorse and pain. His heart whispered to his mind, '*Bouthakrun...*'

A deep sense of separation saddened him, but his mind whispered back to his heart, '*Perhaps, you shall have many more stories to tell, when you return!*'

His shaven head, courtesy of his holy-thread ceremony a couple of days ago, felt even lighter than ever. He wondered, '*Perhaps my head is getting ready for the incoming dose of wisdom! I have heard that travel makes a man wise! Maybe, this lightness is an anatomical method within me to prepare for it...*'

The news reached Kadambari with the suddenness of

a bolt of thunder. However, by then, she was a teenage woman. She had developed the ability to camouflage her subtle melancholy within her heart. The childish delights that she had shared with Robi, her pal, had bloomed into frenzies of early youth.

'Good news!' she replied while being busy with her flowerpots, as Robi stood behind her with a visibly sardonic face. She added, 'Don't look so sad. I know you crave this trip! Sometimes, it's alright to leave behind everything and go. Don't look unhappy, because you're happy within!'

Robi stood speechless while she commented playfully, 'At least I will get some respite from your constant bantering! Now go and prepare for your journey...'

'Alright!' replied Robi with a raised voice. He didn't expect a ruthless response.

As he turned to hurry away, Kadambari softly asked from behind, 'How long would you be away?'

'I don't know!' replied Robi angrily and went away.

She answered back crossly, 'Good! I can now breathe freely for a few months.'

Her words echoed within her room on the roof and then dissipated away. A drop of tear oozed through the edge of her eyes. With a flip of her eyelashes, she made it disappear. The tangy taste of their quarrels always lingered in her heart and made her smile and cry.

Maybe she was lonely. Maybe she was sad. Maybe she was foolish. Only she knew it, no one else...

Soon, the day of departure arrived. Debendranath assembled the entire family in the prayer hall for the customary divine service. Robi had received a full suit of clothes, his first ever, solely for his trip. Debendranath had himself selected their pattern and design. His shaven head was still bald, and he had been given a gold-embroidered velvet cap. He was supposed to cover his head with that ethereal headgear.

Robi boarded the carriage with his father. A final peep at the veranda of the inner chambers brought in a glimpse of Kadambari, who stood at a corner. In that moment of imminent yet temporary separation, a sight flashed passed Robi's eyes...

A little girl dressed in a traditional wedding saree walked upon the marble floor with her soft and naive footsteps, as she shyly tried to hide her face behind the half-drawn veil. Maybe she noticed the little boy standing afar, or maybe she didn't; nobody knew. For a moment, she halted and lifted her eyes from behind her veil.

Robi got into the carriage, and Debendranath said, 'Put on your cap.'

With sheer obedience, he followed the order and sat. Within him, a bizarre concoction of emotions played ruckus.

The Voyage of Enlightenment

First Halt: Bolpur, West Bengal.

The train sped on across the vast rural expanses of Bengal and reached Bolpur in the evening. In the fading twilight, Robi and Debendranath boarded the palanquin to reach their estate. Robi closed his eyes just to avoid a sight of the coveted land of red soil. It was the first time he had visited Bolpur, and Robi wanted to witness the magical beauty of the landscape in the freshness of the new morning!

The land of sandy red soil, the vast stretches of ploughed deep furrows, the miniature mounds of red gravels and pebbles, and the boundless beauty of serene natural abundance filled his heart with an ecstasy that he had always craved for.

At night, he felt annoyed: '*I am enjoying the beauty of the bountiful countryside, while Bouthakrun is alone at home! How can I be so selfish? How is it that I am not sad for my pal? How am I so happy?*'

The questions were pertinent. Yet, the answers were redundant. They were questions that didn't need an answer. They were questions that didn't deserve an answer. It was a phase of life where the heart evolves. There was nothing right or wrong that could be defined as a verdict.

To Robi's sheer surprise, Debendranath didn't restrict him from exploring his freedom. Despite being a strict disciplinarian, he allowed his young child to discover the wonders around those rural settings. Robi had never met his father the way he saw him during those days.

In his innocent heart, Debendranath seamlessly metamorphosed into Baba.

During those wonderful days at Bolpur, Robi roamed around the wildly beautiful landscape like a meandering stream and engaged himself in collecting many curious pieces of stones and gravel.

One evening, Debendranath asked Robi with a childish demeanour, 'How wonderful. Wherever did you get all these?'

An excited Robi replied with a burst of excitement,

'There are many more, thousands and thousands! I could bring as many every day.'

'That would be nice!' replied Debendranath. 'Why not decorate my little hill with them?'

Perhaps the formal barrier between a father and his son was broken that evening. Or, perhaps a bond of love was born in that fading twilight.

Second Halt: Amritsar, Punjab Province.
March 1873.

After departing from Bolpur, they proceeded on an extensive tour. They made short halts at Sahebgunj, Dinapur, Allahabad and Kanpur. Then they reached Amritsar.

The month-long stay at Amritsar had an extensive spiritual impact upon the evolving heart of little Robi.

One morning, Debendranath took Robi to the Gurudarbar of the Sikhs. It was the Durbar Sahib, the Golden Temple of Amritsar. The two entered the serenely beautiful complex. The predominant silence, amidst the breaking dawn, created a magical aura around the young mind of the child. Beside the sprawling lake, the Gurudarbar appeared as a mammoth epitome of a nameless almighty power.

Debendranath took Robi, and the two sat among the multitude of worshippers. Robi looked at him and whispered, 'Baba, what do we do now?'

Debendranath gestured to him to remain quiet and observe. Robi's eyes floated around the collection of buildings around the sanctum and the sacred pool. He looked at the multitude of worshippers seated tranquilly all around. To let the unfolding vibes seep in, he closed his eyes and relaxed his body. Then, the sombre voice of his Baba echoed in the harmony of the devotional hymn. His heart felt blissful, and he silently held his father's hand, while they took a deep breath together.

That day, the Sikh devotees gifted them with sanctified offerings of sugar crystals and other sweetmeats. Robi felt ecstatic, and the same routine followed for many more mornings to come. Somewhere within those pure tunes of the hymns, Robi discovered a freedom of expression through melody. The *Gur-Bani* and *Nanak-Bani* were, imaginably, the triggers that germinated a poetic soul within him at a very young age. Yet, above everything else, once again, it strengthened the bond between a father and a son.

Third Halt: Dalhousie Hills, Himalayas.
April 1873.

The journey into the lofty Himalayas made Robi a vagabond who craved for bottomless beauty. The onward journey through the terraced hills, amid the colourful, blooming flora and fauna of the new spring, awed his youthful heart. Beginning with a simple breakfast of milk and bread, the journeys continued through the ruggedly beautiful mountains until they arrived at a staging bungalow to spend the night. The travels on the customary *Jhamphan* were adventurous escapades for him as he observed the changing beauty of the hills.

During a stay at a halting bungalow, as evening unfolded the approaching night, Debendranath arranged two chairs for them. Robi sat beside his Baba as the dusky twilight gradually faded away and the clear sky became speckled with stars!

Debendranath turned towards Robi and said, 'Look, the assembly of immeasurable stars above have a pattern. Just like the chaos in human lives has a pattern, so do the galaxies beyond our Earth. Let me tell you something about those stars and the constellations...'

At Bakrota, the bungalow was on the highest hilltop. In the freezing cold, Robi woke up one night and, through the open, uncurtained window, saw the shimmering snowy peaks of the mountains, dimly lit in the starlight. The ethereal sight created a melancholic turmoil in him.

'Bouthakrun, I want to write letters to you,' he cried within his heart and subconscious mind. 'Yet, I cannot. Perhaps, when I grow up, I will have the liberty to do so.'

That morning, or rather before dawn, Debendranath finished his early worship and sat beside Robi to wake him up, before sunrise. What followed was a deep spiritual exercise of Sanskrit declensions and then chanting from the Upanishads.

Then came the morning milk and the strenuous walk through the mountains, and finally a bath in the icy cold water! Then, after sessions of spiritual and educational exercises, Robi got an opportunity to wander off into the wilderness of the Himalayas, with a staff in hand, to relish the untamed beauty of Mother Nature.

Then, in the evening, he sat with his Baba again and sang aloud in the Behaag Raag to relieve his spirit into the realms of peace and devotion.

This became a routine in the Himalayas, and somewhere within those breathtaking, solitary journeys, Robi unknowingly became a storyteller.

With the unequivocal knowledge from Peter Parley's

books, hymns of Sanskrit, Proctor's Popular Astronomy and volumes of Gibbon's Rome, he became a learned child of biographies, history, astronomy, modern science and Sanskrit, and conversant in classical poetry of Kalidasa. It redefined the human soul within him, at an early age, and made him wise!

After months of travel, Robi did gain an ethereal wisdom. But to his young soul, he was brimming with stories. Within his heart and mind, he felt proud. Yes, he too could tell his own tales to the entire world.

Inside his own tales of travel, he did perhaps metamorphose into Abdul the sailor!

Robi returned to Tagore Mansion with a shine.

To the entire household and to his Bouthakrun, he now had something to say! He felt special.

She looked at his radiant face, after so many months, and said softly, 'Ribhu, the radiance, has arrived unnoticed...'

Yes, Robi's heart evolved into a vagabond traveller in search of true love.

Bhanusingha—The Rebellious Sun

'Love is an endless mystery, because there is no reasonable cause that could explain it...'

The little boy, the overlooked Robi, found a new place within the inner apartment of the ladies, especially within the quarters of his mother, Sarada Devi. And for Dinu the domestic goldsmith, Pari, the maid, the anonymous carder sitting and cleaning the mattress (and stuffing it on his twanging bow)...the insignificant boy gained a new identity.

'*Don't you dare to ignore me! I am a well-travelled man! I have seen more of this world than you have. I am wiser than you are, so you can no longer disregard my existence!*' were the words that remained unspoken within his mind, while Robi lent them a confident smirk.

On the second day after his return, Robi sat inside the room on the roof with his favourite companion. His homecoming from the travel was not just an arrival; it was a return from his exile in the unnoticed corners of the servants' quarters to a proper place within the inner apartments of the colossal Tagore Mansion. It was a return to the dignity of a grossly overlooked child.

'Bouthakrun, my absence might have kept me out of your mind, but now I have come back in view, and you cannot ignore me!' grinned Robi as he sat and ate the sweetmeats prepared by Kadambari.

'Well, the globetrotter had also not bothered to worry while he was away,' replied Kadambari. 'I was expecting a letter, at least one, maybe!'

'Bouthakrun, the chains of rigorous regime and my own apprehensions had prevented me from doing so!' replied Robi, as he gulped down the delicacies. 'Baba was always unknown to me and I couldn't... But I promise, if ever I go away for long, I shall never refrain from sending you a letter.'

'It's fine! But what did you get for me?' she coaxed him. 'Look, I didn't forget to prepare your favourite food. Now what about you?'

A veil of melancholy descended upon Robi's countenance. He got up quietly, held Kadambari's hand and said, 'Come...'

They walked down the stairs, while the fading twilight flooded the Tagore Mansion with a crimson hue. They entered the sprawling veranda and reached a corner. A metallic trunk sat motionlessly in that corner, amid other redundant objects.

Robi sat down, opened the trunk and took out a cloth bag. He unknotted the bag, took out the contents and placed them on Kadambari's hands. There were a few pieces of colourful gravel and pebbles, and a few folded pages of a notebook.

'This is my treasure and I have kept them for you,' said Robi softly. 'I had secretly written some letters, but didn't get the courage or had the money to post them. Bouthakrun, when I came back, I felt ashamed to give them to you...'

Kadambari snatched away the stash and interrupted Robi with a voice that reverberated inside the corner of the veranda, 'These are gems for me! I am taking them with me.'

As she walked away, Robi stood speechless, while a sweet pang invisibly pierced his bosom.

Within days after his return, Robi metamorphosed into a young prodigy of the inner apartments, particularly in the eyes of his mother, Sarada Devi. She became a proud mother of a boy who had eventually returned as a learned soul, literally.

In the open-air gathering on the parapet-surrounded roof of the inner apartment, Robi was the principal speaker, amid the congregation of ladies. Sun rays fell directly upon the serene roof terrace, and during the daytime, it was used for preparing lemons for pickling. However, as the evening arrived, it transformed into a haunt for the women, who sat with brass vessels containing *kalai* to make pulse-balls, while the air became resonant with gossip. The maidservants were the bearers of that coveted news, while the green mangoes were dried to make delectable *amsi*, or a young jackfruit was sacrificed to become a tangy pickle.

As the Catechu scented with fragrant screw pine filled the air with an intoxicating aroma, Robi took centre-stage to prove that despite his tender age, he had garnered a considerable amount of knowledge within him.

'Look above at those twinkling stars, the millions and billions of gems across the infinite sky, while I reveal to you their astronomical odds and ends, as noted by the famous Proctor...' continued Robi with an air of confidence.

The ladies and the other kids turned their heads and looked up with awe, while the oration of the overenthusiastic boy commenced. Kadambari looked at him and smirked playfully.

Nonetheless, the moment of glory got elevated to a zenith, as Robi and the other children entered the bedroom, where their enormous bedstead lay stretched beside the bed of Sarada Devi herself. In the dim glow of the earthen lamp, she sat in front of them, while her little son reflected a fresh radiance.

'While the others are content with Krittvasa's Bengali rendition of the Ramayana, I have been reading with Baba the original Maharshi Valmiki's Sanskrit version. Maa, I have learnt it on my own in the Himalayas!' added Robi with self-assurance.

'Read me some of that Ramayana, do!' she said in an elated voice.

As the others of tender age sat perplexed at his dexterity, Robi displayed his oratory skills once again within the four walls of that bedroom, which seemed to have metamorphosed into a dreamy opera for him.

'You must read it to Dwijendra! Your elder brother would be really proud of you,' she said ecstatically, as Robi completed a verse.

The balloon of confidence got pricked suddenly, and Robi discharged a baffled grin. In that complex emotional turmoil of panic and inhibition, he hugged his mother (hoping that she would spare him the upcoming embarrassment) and quickly went to sleep.

As the earthen lamps got extinguished, Robi silently prayed for a miracle for himself.

Alas, the jolt of destiny came quite unnoticed.

Sarada Devi had been ailing for quite a long time. However, amid that huge family tree within the Tagore Mansion, none really bothered. She was the wife of Debendranath Tagore, yet her identity remained shrouded within the thick walls of the mansion. So, in an overlooked and unseen course of her existence, her malady took a fatal turn.

The family physician arrived and prescribed her the healing pills. However, nothing much happened. Soon, her condition deteriorated further. For Robi, it was a painful episode. His Maa was a person in whose eyes he had always dreamt of being famous. Despite her separate bed within the same bedroom, she had an aura of affection for her little child. Yet, the slow evaporation of her existence was truly painful.

Then, one day, she was taken away for a boat trip over the Ganges. It was the last option for her revival, perhaps. A troubled Robi asked, 'Bouthakrun, why are they taking Maa away for a boat trip? What is wrong with her? Will she come back home?'

Kadambari wiped away the specs of tears from the brink of Robi's eyes and replied softly, 'Don't worry, she will come back home, soon...'

His prayers and her forecasts were not false. Sarada Devi did come back, but her health failed to heal. A separate room on the third floor of the inner apartments was arranged for her. Again, Robi's young heart failed to comprehend the meaning of that.

Then, one night she passed away.

Yes, it came with suddenness. On the fateful night, Robi and the other kids were fast asleep inside their bedroom when the old nurse came inside, weeping and howling.

As the children woke up with a shock, she moaned, 'Oh my little ones, you have lost your all.'

Kadambari rushed in, rebuked her and led her away. But the apprehension upon her demeanour was visibly evident. Even though no words were spoken, Robi's heart sank into a deep abyss within him. As he reclined his head upon the pillow, he could feel that the cloth cover became more and more wet with the passage of time.

Then, the next morning, Robi and the others were told, 'Maa is no more. She is dead. She passed away last night...'

The words became a distant din while Robi stood on the veranda and witnessed the lifeless body of his Maa stretched upon a wooden bedstead in the courtyard. Nothing in her appearance revealed that death was terrible. The little boy stared at her face. The calmness and tranquillity showed that perhaps she was relieved of all her pains.

His heart whispered to his soul, 'Maa is finally sleeping. Her sleep is simple...'

The gulf between life and its absence was not very conspicuous. Yet, when the hearse got lifted and the corpse got taken away, the eternal absence of his Maa, and the thought that she would never return, made him somewhat unnerved.

Then, before his instability could uproot his sanity, a soft hand held him. In an overwhelmed and muddled voice, Robi could only utter, 'Bouthakrun...'

As the cremation got completed and everyone returned home, Robi stood by his usual corner in the veranda and pondered, 'Maa would never return by this door and take her customary place in the household...'

As the evening grew darker, Robi sulked and walked back. At a moment, he stood and looked up at the house, towards his father's room on the third floor. With a blend of awe and heartbreak, he saw his Baba sitting still on the front veranda, motionless in his prayers.

As he came near his room, a tender voice spoke while a soothing figure emerged from within the darkness. It was Kadambari. She herself was young too, but the world had made her into a mature woman. She touched his shoulders softly and said, 'I shall never let you be lonely…'

As if in a trance, Robi's eyes turned towards the obscure darkness of the bedroom, where a bleak earthen lamp still strived to create luminescence. In that haze, for a brief moment, he saw the face of his Maa. She nodded her head smilingly, as if in agreement and then whispered to him, 'Yes…'

That magical moment vanished too soon. But a strange bond of a nameless love perhaps germinated between two souls, once again. Many years later, a poem spoke from his heart. Maybe it did evolve in that magical moment…

I cannot remember my mother,
Only sometimes in the midst of my play
A tune seems to hover over my playthings,
The tune of a song that she used to
Hum while rocking my cradle.

I cannot remember my mother,
But when in the early autumn morning

The smell of the Shiuli flowers floats in the air;
The scent of the morning service in the
Temple comes to me as the scent
Of my mother.

~

Time waits for none. Thus, the healing touch of oblivion blew in with the passage of time, even though melancholy lingered in Robi's heart, somewhere.

Jyotirindranath brought the winds of sophistication into the household. His creative bent of mind percolated in his choices. Under his instruction, a piano arrived in the terrace room. During the evenings, he sat on the terrace with his violin and played sweet melodies while Robi sat beside him and absorbed the beauty in those tunes.

With time, the teenage ushered into Robi. The joy of growing up together, experiencing the onset of adolescence and tasting the first dews of youth... everything created a timeless attachment between the young souls of his Bouthakrun and him.

Jyotirindranath took it upon himself to groom Kadambari in many facets. He encouraged her into education, and she became a voracious reader. He taught her horse riding too. Robi sat upon the veranda and watched them while Kadambari went riding a horse along the Chitpore Road. Nonetheless, somewhere she was lonely. The companionship of a life-partner was lost in the fatherly affection from her husband.

However, with Robi, she felt an unnamed elation!

During a hot summer noon, as Robi returned home

for lunch, Kadambari placed a plate in front of him and served fresh hot shrimp curry with rice. Robi gorged upon the food while his senses absorbed the culinary charm. His voice could only utter, 'Bouthakrun, this is ethereal…'

She was a fantastic cook, and she took pride in cooking for him. She replied light-heartedly, 'A good cook is always dexterous at everything!'

'Oh really?' replied Robi. 'Then let us combat in a game of chess after I finish my meal. I shall prove that a connoisseur of good food is equally dexterous!'

During that lazy afternoon, she defeated him every time in the game of chess and criticized him for his playful stubborn notions: 'I told you that I will win every bet!'

'Bouthakrun, you are like a sorcerer! I shall name you Hecate, the Greek goddess of sorcery and witchcraft. This is humanly impossible.'

Kadambari sat upon the bed with a radiant face while Robi continued, 'I have written a poem. Would you read it?'

'No, you read it out to me,' she replied.

As Robi held his notebook in his hands and orated his lines, Kadambari listened to him with closed eyes. Then, as he finished and looked at her, she teased him with the words, 'No. You are not even half as good as Behari Chakraborty! I don't think you can ever get even an inch closer to his finesse.'

A visibly cross Robi replied, 'You shall never be able to understand my poetry! It is useless to demonstrate in front of you.'

As he paced out of the room, her voice echoed back,

'Pain... A depiction of pain is essential. It is what makes a poem immortal. Every poem must infuse an anecdote of a melancholic mood that must linger on and on...'

Robi smiled back. Perhaps he understood. He didn't reply. He nodded his head and then went away.

She was the magician in his life! She crafted him and his persona and chiselled the deep emotional epitome within him. The sensitive bond he shared with Kadambari perhaps blossomed through the ecstasy in his joy of creating magnificent words.

One afternoon, Robi stood beside the parapet of the roof and asked, 'Bouthakrun, my collection of poems is coming off nicely. But I need a pen name for myself! Can you suggest one?'

Kadambari looked at him, smiled and said, 'We must all discover a name for our own selves! I can criticize your works, but you must name yourself from the bottom of your heart.'

She held his hands and added, 'Close your eyes and churn out the name for the bard who is about to be born... He is your unborn inner child. Give him a drop of your own blood and bring him to life!'

Robi listened to her words that had a deep-rooted meaning. Then, he closed his eyes and transported his heart into the depths of his soul. A few moments later, with spontaneous energy, he cried, '*Bhanusingha*! Yes... The Sun-Lion! Robi shall be reborn as Bhanusingha, an ancient Vaishnava poet. My works would come out as the lost works of a long-forgotten, but newly discovered poet. You always tell me that I have an ancient soul. The poems would be a tribute to that ancient poet.'

'Very well,' replied Kadambari. Melancholy gripped

her mood. She said, 'But I believe, your own name, Rabindranath Tagore, would outshine everything else! Rabindranath, the Lord of the Rebellious Sun. I believe, one day you shall no longer be ancient. You shall become timeless!'

At the age of sixteen, Robi released his first collection of poems under the pseudonym Bhanusingha, chronicling the divine love of Radha and Krishna. Through his verses, the Rebellious Sun immortalized the nameless purity of love within his soul. She was his inspiration and the first person who lent him confidence.

Jyotirindranath used to have his morning coffee arranged in the staircase room on the eastern side of the terrace. Young Robi was often a companion for his brother in that room where Jyotirindranath engaged his heart and mind inside the depths of his literary creations. Despite the age difference of twelve long years, to his Jyotidada he was an equal sibling.

'Listen to this', said Jyotirindranath one morning. 'It is the first draft of a new play.'

As he orated, Robi listened silently. Then, after a while, Jyotirindranath asked, 'Robi, the conversation between the protagonist and his muse seems a bit blank. Can you add something to it?'

Kadambari came in quietly and stood behind her husband. Robi closed his eyes and poured his heart into a brief input. Then, as he opened his eyes and looked at her, a soft smile embraced her countenance.

Jyotirindranath added with fervour, 'It is perfect! Robi, your wild spirit brings so much vibrancy to it!'

Robi sat and soaked in the appreciation. He felt happy to be the co-creator for his talented brother, and the moment of glory was too precious.

'I am formally inducting you into the editorial board of *Bharati*. Robi, I want you to refine your critical piece on Michael Madhusudan Dutta's *Meghnadbadh Kavya*. I think it will be a fantastic write-up for the first issue!'

Robi felt overexcited. He had been very confident about his creation.

'I think it is too amateurish to be a candidate for the first issue,' commented Kadambari. 'Criticism must be impudent and speak vividly! It can never be disrespectful, yet it must create a visible contrast in the minds of the readers. That piece needs a lot of rework.'

The subtle pride in Robi's eyes evaporated instantaneously. He managed to gather his senses and replied, 'I shall work on it more. Jyotidada, give me some time, and I will perfect the piece so that it is worthy of being published in the first issue of *Bharati*.'

Kadambari was his severest critic and did not let him get carried away by the excitements of his early creations. Robi realized that but vowed to himself, silently, 'Bouthakrun, one day I shall shine in the glitters of the dark pupils of your eyes!'

As the teenage years reached their prime, Robi too became deeply engrossed with his Jyotidada and Bouthakrun. The beauty in their relationship bloomed, and the fragrance filled their senses.

Umesh, a smart vendor, started coming to the Tagore household with his fashionable booty collected from English shops for the ladies of the household. Robi abhorred that attire. He loved his Bouthakrun in her traditional enigma.

One evening, he expressed his dislike in front of

Kadambari by saying, 'I hate these items that represent the very latest fashion!'

'Don't be cheeky', she replied and went inside. Before going, she added, 'Wait here. I want to show you something.'

A few minutes later, Kadambari came out, draped in a beautiful silk saree, inadvertently bought from the collection of Umesh. She stood in front of Robi and asked, 'How is it?'

Robi looked at her silently, then replied dryly, 'Bouthakrun, you look fine in it. However, the old-fashioned black-bordered white sarees, or even the ones from Dhaka, are far better and more tasteful.'

Kadambari laughed and replied, 'You surely are an old man!'

Robi rebelled, 'The modern women dressed in georgette sarees with their faces painted like dolls are guilty of forgery in their dresses and their complexions!'

'That means even I am guilty of that same guiltiness!' she added with an air of scorn.

'No... I mean,' fumbled Robi, 'Bouthakrun, you look far better than them. Yet, I don't consent to the choices of fashion these days.'

'You are ancient!' she finished.

Robi never really succeeded in beating her in an argument. Her answers were never governed by the purview of logic, and Robi willingly accepted that fact.

~

Jyotirindranath played a vital role in the personal and literary development of Robi. Being an ardent companion of his brother, Robi, at times, even accompanied him during trips. It was one such trip that remained etched in the recollections of the young man.

On a placid monsoon weekend, Jyotirindranath, Kadambari and Robi travelled to the beautiful garden house of the Tagore family in Chandannagar. The picturesque, two-storied villa, nestled within the bounty of Mother Nature along the banks of the Ganges.

Upon arrival, Kadambari threw herself into the depths of the culinary endeavours while Jyotirindranath sat down with his favourite violin. It was a damp and humid evening, with an overburden of rainclouds and a complete absence of showers. Robi sat beside him and listened to the tune, while he sipped his cool lemon juice. The shores of the Ganges were the undisturbed haunts of birds and insects. A light breeze from the rippling waters brought in the fragrance of the semi-moist soil.

A sumptuous dinner was served soon, and they finished their meals. The night was not very eventful, courtesy of the tiring day, and they went back to their rooms. Amid the rural settings, away from the humdrum of the city, Jyotirindranath too wanted a respite of tranquillity.

That night, as Robi reclined upon his bed, the sweet oblivion of sleep took him into a world of dreams. Then, an unknown song filled his senses...

Silently, the night cried. Silently, the eyes sighed.
Yet, the silence had a relentless voice. In that silence, there was always a choice.
Silently, the day had faded her light. Silently, his heart had become quiet.
In silence, his sleep came. In silence, his dreams became...

Yes, it was a dream in which he became the same little boy that he was before his mother died.

As the sleepy hollow took him deeper into the depths of the dream, he saw a blissful morning of a beautiful monsoon day. As the rains came down, Robi's eyes beheld her…his Maa. She was sitting in her favourite room inside the garden house, as a playful Robi carelessly ran across the long veranda, without paying much attention.

In a strange concoction of emotions, his heart wept, 'Maa? Is that you? How is that possible? Maa, is that really you?'

Robi ran back to the door and peeped inside. With an unutterable longing, he looked and saw that it was indeed her. Through the tinted glass of the window panes, the smooth colours of the tranquil sunlight surrounded her with the hues of the rainbow. As confusion and ecstasy coagulated together, he rushed down to her and touched her feet with his forehead.

Maa held his hands softly, looked into his eyes and said, 'You have come! Robi…'

Then the dream broke…

As Robi opened his eyes into the harsh world of reality, he comprehended that he was dreaming. The showers had commenced outside the garden house, and the raindrops were dancing upon the rooftop. In that sweet melancholy, his soul yearned for a glimpse, for a touch of his Maa, and to hear her sweet voice.

The morning was beautiful, and Robi walked up the stairs and reached the rooftop. Above, the proud rainclouds gathered like an army that bestowed their shadows upon the soft earth, the rippling Ganges, the relentless shore and beyond into the jungle.

Robi didn't compose a song of his own. Instead, he sang aloud—'*Bhara Badara Maha Badara Sunya Mandira Mor...*'

He moulded those lines into his own melody and created heartfelt music in his own voice as the raindrops drenched him and the gust of winds swept through the trees across the shore and entangled their branches with each other, while they seemed to dance to his ethereal song.

The song floated in the wind and touched a heart. It was the heart of Kadambari. She too ran up the stairs and stood by the shade beside the parapet. She stood like a stone and watched him sing. But she didn't utter a word. Robi stopped and looked at her, while the rain poured across his body and drenched him. Then, he slowly went downstairs, while she stood there quietly.

As the sounds of his footsteps dissolved away, she stepped into the rain, under the open sky. The madness of the showers drenched her too, while she softly swirled in a dance, alone! Her face turned up towards the lofty sky and her eyes closed in a dreamy haze...

Whether Jyotirindranath witnessed that euphoria, no one knew. Maybe it was not necessary to be known.

Then, at age seventeen, it was decided by his father that Robi must go to England to become a barrister. The jolt of fate meant to separate him from his beloved Bouthakrun.

The desolate, shy young man, the Rebellious Sun, the young Bhanusingha, was all set to be uprooted from the soil of love.

Ghare-Baire
The Home and The World

Drishti—When the Eyes Met

'Music fills the infinite between two souls...'

The verdict arrived from Debendranath and percolated through the voices of his descendants. It reached the tender auditory organs of Robi with a ruthlessness. '*It is the desire of Baba that you must travel to England for your further education. There, you would have an opportunity to become a successful barrister.*'

Quietly, Robi gulped down the decree, as it continued to crash upon him. '*Initially, that is, before sailing for England, you shall spend a few months with your Mejodada. Satyendranath is alone in Ahmedabad, and he would be a perfect mentor to groom you in English mannerisms. Once he gets a furlong to travel to England and be with his family, you shall accompany him and sail together.*'

'*There is not much time. Begin the preparations for your journey. You must travel to Ahmedabad at the earliest to be with your Mejodada.*' This completed the announcement of the verdict...

Satyendranath had met his father, the stalwart Maharshi Debendranath, and had convinced him about the future of his little brother, who was approaching his adulthood. The result of the discussion was the verdict.

'I have left the editorial board of *Bharati*,' said a visibly upset Robi. 'My job is done. The literary endeavours must culminate now.'

'I feel as if I am being torn up by the roots from my beloved soil and being planted in an alien land with an equally alien atmosphere!' sighed Robi, as he stood on the open roof and rested his arms upon the parapet.

The wintry breeze floated the chills around while the clear night sky flaunted the sparkling shimmers of the countless stars. Clad in a warm Kashmiri shawl, Robi stood and stared at that eternal infinity and added, 'Bouthakrun, I don't aspire to become a barrister. Then, why do I have to go? Why is it so that we have to live someone else's dream? Why...?'

Kadambari stood beside him, while the melancholy condensed into a soft layer of fog upon the public pond beyond the Tagore Mansion. She said softly, 'Look at the stars. They are twinkling so vibrantly. Yet, when the day breaks, they become invisible. However, they are not gone. The day obscures their perceptibility but can never eradicate their existence.'

Robi looked at her silently. His eyes were tearful, but he didn't speak. She added, 'Your dreams are like those infinite constellations of stars! Even if the brightness of life's verdict camouflages their existence, they are very much real, and they are inevitable parts of your life's universe! Robi, the Rebellious Sun, might burn to shower light upon the world, but the stars of his own dreams would always be behind him, twinkling brightly in his own sky. A day will come when your dreams will be dreamt by the entire world.'

'Bouthakrun, do you believe so?' asked Robi. 'Would you dream those dreams too?'

Kadambari smiled shyly and replied, 'Yes... Now please stop brooding and prepare for your voyage! And this time, I won't spare you if you don't write me letters!'

'I will not make that mistake again!' laughed Robi. He felt relieved. 'I don't know how long I will be away from home. I don't know how much I will be able to fulfil those weird dreams. However, at least I will get to see some new places!'

As Robi walked away, the grandfather clock gonged to usher in the hour before midnight. Kadambari went inside her bedroom. Jyotirindranath was not home yet. He was spending the night for the rehearsal of his new opera.

Kadambari extinguished the lamps and reclined upon the huge bed. The melancholic fog had unknowingly floated above the waterbody outside the Tagore Mansion and snuck inside her room. Beside her bed was a terracotta flower-vase, upon which she had kept a bunch of *rajnigandha* (tuberoses).

The heavenly fragrance of the nocturnal bloom created an aura of romance in her solitary heart, and she hummed with a smile. They were her own words...

The twinkling stars, above
Spoke to her on the lone cold night,

The breeze whispered songs of love
When there was darkness in her sight,

Her giggles and tears mingled to smear
Into the depths of an emotional lair,

Then she shrieked with a colossal ecstasy
Her silent cry was a fragrant fantasy,

As the dawn peeped through the horizon
Her soul sank in a melancholic ocean,

Blossom of the Night was but a Queen
To her, a new day was always unseen...

Then, she closed her eyes and whispered to her own soul, 'Yes, the Blossom of the Night is never destined to bloom in the light of the Rebellious Sun! She can, but leaves her fragrance behind, for the new dawn.'

The preparations were done, and soon the day of departure came near. The blooming young man with a poetic heart was all set to start his journey into the outer world. Nonetheless, for the second time in his life, he experienced a strange emotion. Yet, there was something different this time. Ever since his childhood, the lonely boy wanted to feel the breeze of freedom. However, at the moment of bidding farewell to his Bouthakrun, he felt a prick in his heart. He feared that the way ahead was unknown, treacherous and companionless.

On the morning of his departure, he met Kadambari and placed a notebook in her hands. He said, 'Goodbye, Bouthakrun. However, I am giving you my most precious possession. It is the notebook in whose pages my first verses germinated. Keep it safe for me. I shall return and take it back from you. While you take care of it, this notebook and the words etched in her pages will take care of you...'

Kadambari smiled. Then, she held the notebook close to her bosom while her Robi went away.

Palatial Mansion, Shahibagh. Ahmedabad, Gujarat. March 1878.

The journey across the heart of the country, stretching from the East to the West, was his first rendezvous with the Western frontier. As the train dashed over the railway lines, the metallic clatter of the accelerating wheels created a banter which kept reverberating within his mind. However, the changing face of Mother Nature, with the passage of the miles, breathed in a freshness into his heart. Hence, with a strange blend of detachment and discovery playing ruckus within his soul, Robi sat inside the compartment as it jingled away through the rural vastness.

Then, the train arrived at its final destination and introduced Robi to Ahmedabad.

'*Everything is so different,*' wondered Robi, as he headed towards his new abode. '*The people and their clothes, their mannerisms and their dialect, everything is so contrasting. Will I ever be able to acclimatize myself to the diversity?*'

As the camel-driven carriage reached Shahibagh, Robi alighted from the vehicle to glance upon the huge palatial mansion in front of him. The mammoth structure silenced him.

'*This is like a colossal prehistoric monster standing silently like a statue in front of the Sabarmati River! Within its belly, it perhaps hides so many mysteries...*' he wondered.

His trance was broken by the sound of a familiar voice. 'Robi, my boy, I am so glad to get this opportunity to spend some quality time with you!'

Satyendranath Tagore, Robi's second brother, was a Judge of the Bombay Presidency and was posted in Ahmedabad. An able Civil Servant of the Imperial Government, he was a man of liberal temperament and an open mind. He was almost two decades older than Robi, but his rebellious nature and his broadminded worldview made him a worthy confidante.

'Finally, you have been able to come out from the confines of the Tagore Mansion to witness the evolution of the outer world!' exclaimed Satyendranath.

'Mejodada, this looks like a fortress. It overshadows even our Jorashako house!' replied Robi with a smile.

The scorching summer of Ahmedabad was yet to set in. However, the sweet chill of Bengal's winter was missing in the air. The pricking dryness in the winds lent a different sensation to the skin. Altogether, Robi felt soberly content.

'Yes, let us go inside,' replied Satyendranath. 'These judges' quarters are but the former palaces of the Mughal kings. This palace is beautiful. Located by the Sabarmati River, it brings in a soft, refreshing aura to the inhabitants. Look at that veranda, what do you think about it?'

The wide terrace stretched modestly across the palace and commanded a picturesque view of the Sabarmati, whose knee-deep water meandered through the sands.

'It is different, but it is beautiful...' replied Robi.

That night, the brothers finished their dinner and sat upon the open roof. The manservants arranged two armchairs and some refreshments. They faced the open vastness that extended across the riverbed and beyond into the forest. The desert had beautifully blended with the greenery to give a rugged exquisiteness that glittered like silver in the soft moonlight.

'You know, Robi, I always believed that the *purdah* system in our family is not that of our own nation, but a copy of some other culture! My visit to England opened my mind and established my beliefs even more strongly. There, I witnessed so much freedom for women! It is a social necessity. It helped me understand the relatively poor position of women in our Indian society. I am sure your voyage to England would provide you with a vision that would be much more liberal and would help you discover the truth of real freedom,' said Satyendranath.

It was a deeply emotional moment, and Robi understood the turmoil his Mejodada had witnessed. He was aware of the desperate audacity that the man had displayed, and he felt happy in his company. He replied, 'Ever since my childhood, I had not spent much time with you, Mejodada. Today, under the moonlit sky, I feel excited to listen to you.'

Satyendranath patted him on his shoulder and continued, 'After my marriage, in Jnanadanandini, I found an ideal partner to fulfil my thinking. When I was thrilled about witnessing the progress of women in the advanced society in the West, I wanted to take her to England to experience the same. Sadly, the familial fences are too high for a Bengali boy, but Robi, I have tried and I have revolted, perhaps even a lot, against Baba. It might have saddened him immensely. Maybe that is why I am so detached from my roots. But I am satisfied.'

His words rippled out like a foamy waterfall and overwhelmed Robi's heart. 'I took your *Mejo-Bouthan* with me to Bombay, where she ably tried to live in the manner and style of the wives of the English officers of the Indian Civil Service. Robi, you are too young to maybe understand the complications of society and the conservative family, yet I feel like expressing myself to you. Despite the nineteen years that separate us, tonight you are my closest family here in this barren land! When Jnanadanandini and I once returned to Jorashako for a holiday, we created a sensation in the Calcutta society. I was once invited to a party at the Government House. Breaking all traditional rules, I took Jnanadanandini to accompany me to the party. There she was "...*A lone Bengali woman in the midst of hundreds of English women*!" Ahhhh, what a satisfaction it was! Robi, the feeling of a rebel when he breaks all barriers, is truly ethereal. Many criticized us, but I was content. And in her loving eyes, I was a victor! Maybe a day will come when that freedom will be enjoyed by every woman of our country!'

Robi sipped from the cup of fragrant tea and listened to his Mejodada. It was a night when he was truly meeting his brother, who was, till then, a distant star in the vast galaxy of his stellar family. Satyendranath finished his cup of tea and said, 'Last year, I sent Jnanadanandini and the kids to England, accompanied by an English couple. She went with three children, and while expecting our fourth. Your Mejo-Bouthan is a strong lady. The voyage was indeed a daring task to undertake. But I am happy. Soon, I hope so, we will be able to travel and be united with them.'

Then, as they got up, he added, 'Robi, my boy, I think the almighty has given us this opportunity to know each other. I think this is your unique chance to know the world beyond and extend your spirit into the realms of enlightenment. Be happy and stride ahead.'

The hours that elapsed in the company of his brother left an unmatched impact upon his heart. Robi went to sleep with dreamy eyes and a bubbling heart.

Despite so, Robi was inherently a shy person. Or perhaps, he was an introvert who dreamt of being an extrovert, but not through exquisite expressions. Maybe his extroversion was meant to bloom through his unspoken words. Hence, in that distant city of Ahmedabad, where the language and the culture were unfamiliar, Robi began to cocoon himself. During the daytime, when Satyendranath was away for work, Robi found it difficult to step out and find people to familiarize with. His coy inhibition began to create an unseen fence around him, and he stayed within that heavily secured perimeter.

One afternoon, when Satyendranath was away for work, Robi was all alone in that huge palatial Judge's Quarters. He roamed around on the marbled floors while the sombre wind floated around like an invisible apparition that aspired to seek his attention. Robi ran across the sprawling veranda and the open corridor adjoining the banks of the Sabarmati, in search of those voices to speak with.

He whispered inside the enormous hall, 'Are you there? Can I speak with you? Would you like to talk to me?'

His own voice reverberated across the thick stone walls and created an echo that seemed like a reply in chorus. The vast house seemed like a cavernous emptiness that created an aura of the bygone history. Life in Ahmedabad was different. It was a distinct contrast to what life was like in Bengal. In that dry and warm land, the air was sprinkled with remnants of history which seemed to have frozen in the warp of time.

Robi whispered to himself, '*History has paused in this beautiful portrait of the yesteryears! Life here is standing with her face turned towards her aristocratic past. Her former days are buried in the earth like the treasures of the Jokkho...*'

Robi swirled around to catch a glimpse of those elusive companions. The glittering reflections of the sunlight upon the water of Sabarmati played a game of hide-and-seek with his eyes. He felt amused and giggled, '*I know, you are there. Yes, I know...*'

He stood quietly across the open terrace and contemplated, '*The stone-built tanks scattered along this terrace hold their secrets in their masonry! Yes, those are secrets of the luxurious bathing halls of the Begums!*'

He laughed, '*Begums of the past, I think I know you. Begums of the past, I can feel you. I can sense that you are running across those marble stairs. I can feel you stride into the river while you splash in the games of your ecstatic baths! I can see you while you run by me, drenched in your wet sarees as you head into the secret chambers!*'

Then, he stretched himself upon the floor of the huge hall, extended his limbs and shouted, '*Kshudhita Pashan* (Hungry Stones), *I know you are alive and I shall learn your stories, so that one day I can tell them to the entire world...*'

No, he was not becoming mad. No, he was not in a hallucination. No, he was not in a state of depression and seclusion. Robi was experiencing a state of sheer outburst of creative maturity while being cocooned in that lonely palace. The experience later became a foundation of his literary life.

Surprisingly, in that solitary existence, for Robi life was crazy. Life was remote yet creative. And the destitution created a haunting ghost within his solitary existence. It was a ghost of his own ego that helped him transition into the realm of adulthood. Perhaps that germinated the verses which Robi was later destined to chronicle as a moan against the almighty who had shaped his life...

I was telling you my tale
I was telling you so many stories of my life
You put them to the flames
You drowned them in your tears
This is how you rebuilt me
As an image after Your Heart.

In those days of solitary existence, Robi felt a subtle pain for his detachment from one person who had been his lifelong confidante. She was his Bouthakrun, Kadambari. The nomadic existence and the faint ignorance about the future created turmoil within his heart. One night, he sat down to write a letter.

Bouthakrun,

I am here, yet the vagabond soul of Robi roams across the vast and endless desert in search of an oasis. They say love is blind. Does that mean that to see more is to be blind? For love sharpens the eye and enlarges the understanding.

The difference between friendship and love is that while the former means two persons and the world, the latter means that the two persons are the world. In friendship, one plus one is three; in love, one plus one is one!

In this vast emptiness, I roam around to seek many answers. While in Jorashako, you were there, Bouthakrun, to whisper the answers whenever I felt bewildered. Here, in this Bedouin life, my own voiceless shadow tries hard to do so. Yet, I fail to understand them.

Suffering is another word for obsession with self. That is why the sight of beauty brings joy by taking us away from ourselves.

In this huge remnant of the Mughal architecture, I sit alone beside the banks of the Sabarmati and compose my own songs. At times, the words come first. At times, the tune germinates first.

I don't know when, but the day I return to you, I shall sing them to you. I don't restrict my heart to tell you that there is none in this world, Bouthakrun, who knows the real person who resides in this mortal body.

Yours,
Robi

As he finished writing, Robi read the letter a few times. It made him feel happy. It made him feel closer to his Bouthakrun. However, the arrows of Cupid pricked his sentiments and created a sensation of guilt mingled with gloom. Robi got up onto the bed, came near the flames of the candle and burnt the letter!

As the piece of paper got converted to ashes, a few drops of tears appeared near the brim of his eyes. Robi extinguished the candle with a blow and then closed his eyes, as he reclined his body upon the bed.

'*Perhaps one day, I shall be able to write these lines freely,*' he sighed.

Despite every moment of vulnerability, Robi did write

some letters to his beloved childhood companion. Some of those letters got posted, secretly, while some remained unsent in his own possessions. However, the minutes that he spent composing those letters were moments when he really felt united with her. It was the maturing of a love that was nameless, yet it was a fearless sentiment that bloomed within his heart. However, the shackles of society and the encumbrance of familial bonds made him feel crippled even to try and understand what was brewing within his young heart.

The library at the Judge's Quarters was richly stocked with literary masterpieces. Robi dived into that ocean of literature, and many of his contributions to the *Bharati* magazine reflected the influence of those works in the development of his own self.

At the Tagore Mansion, life had grasped a deep and mellow silence. The loneliness of Kadambari became like a wild ghost that began to haunt her. Robi's absence created a substantial void in her life. Jyotirindranath was more and more involved with his business interest, the business of steamers across the Padma River, and his literary endeavours that began to pull him into the world of theatre and of enigmatic courtesans.

One evening, Kadambari sat by the corner of the huge veranda, as the evening twilight was fading fast. She held the old notebook in her hand and sighed, 'Robi, your notebook is etched with the vibes of your blooming heart. In this huge mansion, those pages speak with me, as my confidante and sparkles up my mood.'

That night, Kadambari wrote a letter to Robi. Her

expressions came out in a beautiful verse... It was a song that perhaps described her in the light of womanhood.

She sang it aloud to herself, as she reclined upon her bed. In the dead of the night, when everyone was asleep, she too became the Bedouin soul in search of her oasis.

In her verses, she lived many a life
In her verses, she died many a death,

In her verses, she smiled many a smile
In her verses, she suffered many an ache,

The poet sat inside her forlorn prison
While the glass panes clouded her vision,

No rain, no sun, ever touched her
The lone poet just wrote in fervour,

Then, when a storm came and broke the window
As the sunlight killed the choking damp mellow,

The poet had lived her curse of life
The poet had died her gift of death...

Alas, Kadambari too never posted the letter. As she read the letter to herself, tears remained her sole companion. Then she tore it apart into pieces. However, the song remained engraved in her heart and mind.

A line that Robi once told her reverberated in her mind, and she said to herself, '*Our ancients say that modesty is a woman's best ornament. But women put on so many ornaments that there is little room left for this one!*'

The question was relevant, but the answer was too audacious!

The destitution of the young man became more and more visible, and Satyendranath understood his mental state. He contemplated the matter and came up with a plan. However, only destiny knew that it was a plan that was preordained to metamorphose the life of Robi.

One evening, after returning from work, Satyendranath summoned him and said, 'Robi, I know that you feel lonely here. I am busy with my work during the entire day and seldom find much time for you. It has been almost four months, and I feel really handicapped that my little brother is struggling with the transition.'

Robi looked at him while Satyendranath continued, 'Thus, I have decided something. It will not only reduce your homesickness but also provide you with an opportunity to familiarize yourself with the etiquette of the English society.'

Robi looked at him silently in anticipation, and he said with a smile, 'You must travel to Bombay. There, you shall stay in the house of Dr Atmaram Pandurang Turkhud. He is a personal friend, and his daughter, Annapurna, has just returned from England after completing her education. I think she would be the perfect person to help you familiarize with the culture of English society. So, get ready for your next destination. I am sure it will be a great experience for you.'

Thus, another momentous juncture unknowingly arrived in the life of the young man. Destiny had a strange plan for his life's journey, and Robi reached the home of Dr Atmaram Pandurang Turkhud. Yet, this was again a very new culture, and Robi was yet to get familiarized with his new environment.

Robi entered through the gate and was ushered

inside by a servant. The beautiful small bungalow had the smoothness and the ease of a relaxed lifestyle. Situated at a little distance from the Bombay beach, the moderately upscale English-style bungalow looked serenely beautiful. The small yet vibrant garden oozed the beauty of colours through its bounty of blossoms. Unconsciously, Robi felt an attachment to the household's vibrancy after the barren ruthlessness of the Mughal palace grounds.

The aged host welcomed Robi with great warmth. Dr Atmaram, a man of handsome manners, greeted him: 'Mr Rabindranath Tagore, welcome to my abode. Your brother had written to me about you and your future aspirations. I am happy that you have chosen such a wonderful path ahead. Please feel absolutely comfortable in this house. My second daughter has just returned from England and is very conversant with the niceties of the English culture and the language. She will be your teacher. Well, I mention the term teacher, but she is just about the same age as yours, and I think she will be like a guide to you and be able to help you.'

'Thank you so much, sir,' replied Robi shyly. 'I am really glad about the arrangements.'

'So, please take a seat on the sofa and be comfortable,' commented Dr Atmaram. 'I will ask the housemaid to fetch you some refreshments, and then you can go upstairs to your room. It is a room that we have chosen for you for a very special reason. I will not reveal the reason. You shall discover it once you enter it.'

Saying those words, Dr Atmaram went inside while Robi wondered what was about to unfold in his own life.

As he stood at a corner of the well-decorated living room, a sweet, feminine voice called him from behind,

'Hello, are you Rabindranath?'

As he turned and beheld her, Robi saw a young girl, groomed in classy English style but with a plethora of simplicity and innocence, staring at him with large, expressive eyes. As their eyes met, Robi remained speechless whilst she smiled softly. Her nicely knotted hair, with a few stray locks floating carelessly over her forehead, interfered with her temporarily questioning sight, while her thin, charming lips throbbed with the echo of the question that she had just uttered.

'Ahhhh, yes,' fumbled Robi after a few moments of enthralled, dumbfounded blankness. 'Yes, I am Rabindranath, but you can call me... Robi.'

Robi was the epitome of vivacious youth. And his eyes, despite his shy demeanour and his ever-downed eyelids, were like the lighthouses of life that could steal the hearts of despondent seamen.

The girl looked at his face with an innocent awe, and then she replied, 'I am Annapurna, but you can call me Anna...'

Nalini—An Epistle of Youth

'Love's gift cannot be given; it waits to be accepted...'

Thus, in Bombay, a vibrant Robi met Annapurna Pandurang Turkhud. As he stood, tall and handsome, Robi was like a gust of fresh air. He was a bouquet of sunlight through the open skylight. He was a man who could mesmerize his beholder. Anna's beautiful hair fluttered in the light breeze as she stood and stared at the attractive charmer. For young Annapurna, aka Anna, he was an irresistible phenomenon! She fell in love with him at first sight!

Within a few moments, she collected her wits and said in a quivering voice, 'Oh, Robi...that is a nice name. I am sure you would have a good time in our house...'

Her eyes gathered a nervousness as she felt a throbbing excitement. That singular moment got picturesquely portrayed in both the young hearts and created a tornado. That moment redefined her conviction, her inner soul and her heart. As if in slow motion, her eyes dared to glimpse into his eyes and steal away the heart of the seventeen-year-old youth!

Contrastingly, in Robi's eyes, she sparkled up as

the epitome of a polished femme, while he himself was an ordinary young man who had very insignificant achievements in life. He was an average boy who had reached adulthood with no great ambition in mind and was somebody whom a lady of her finesse could easily ignore. Hardly did he know what Anna felt within her throbbing heart. The dramatic moment was transient, but for the young hearts, the symphonies of romance commenced their elaborate performances while they dared to look into each other's eyes.

Robi was at a loss for words. Anna was a beautiful tempest that had suddenly stormed into his life, and he was left speechless. To express his mediocre existence with a decent identity, and finding nothing else to say, Robi said blatantly, 'I am a poet. I can write poetry...'

It was his only talent that he could showcase to gain a bit of attention and respect. A scepticism played ruckus in his mind as he fumbled in front of her. He didn't expect a positive response.

Yet, Anna accepted his words with full faith. She smiled through her beautiful, thin lips that seemed to him like two delicate petals of a fresh rose. In his palpitating heart, a subtle turmoil started to play a riot. Kadambari was his constant soul, but Anna was like a gale in his life. Unable to bear the thrust with which she thundered into his entire existence, he was left unnerved.

The exquisite moment was cut short by the re-entry of Dr Atmaram. He came back and said to Robi, 'Your room is ready. Please come upstairs and freshen up.'

Robi returned to reality from the dreamy drama that was slowly unfolding. As he jutted back, he nodded his head obediently and headed upstairs. While walking up, he momentarily turned his head towards the point where Anna was standing still. Yes, she stood there like an exquisitely carved marble statue, and she looked at him with an audacious glance, while a soft smile adorned her countenance.

As Robi entered his room, he saw the huge English-style window overlooking the seashore. Robi went in and then stood in front of the window. As the servants left, he opened the glass windows and the salty wind gusted in. It splashed upon his face, as if it were trying to tell him, '... *Taste the sweet honey of youth. Robi, she is the goddess of your youthful fantasy! There is nothing right or wrong in life. Perhaps, this awry wind of romance will redefine your soul.*'

During tea time in the evening and then subsequently at the dinner table, Robi met the entire family of Dr Atmaram. It was an eloquent family of the accomplished doctor. It comprised his wife, Radhabai, two daughters (Manek and Annapurna) and two sons (Moreshwar and Dhyaneshwar). The highly educated and acclaimed family members were sophisticated in their manners but were simple in their nature. That night, the two sons were not home, but Robi was introduced to the rest of the family.

'Son, what do you think about our Marathi cuisine?' asked Radhabai, as she served a delicacy from her kitchen. 'Does it taste palatable?'

'Oh yes', replied Robi shyly. 'It is very good.'

'Robi, you have ventured out on a long journey. How do you feel about being away from home for such a prolonged period?' asked Dr Atmaram.

'Sir, it is different,' replied Robi in a mellowed voice.

'I have spent most of my life within the Tagore Mansion. Only once, I had been on a tour to the Himalayas with my father, and it was an enchanting journey. I feel a longing for my home. It has been my entire universe, but the escapade into the outer world is equally enriching. At least I will learn something that I can tell the others when I return.'

Manek sat across the table and added mischievously, 'Anna is a very strict teacher! Robi, you'd better be careful. And don't forget your homework, or else she will make you rework for hours!'

A purple tinge appeared across Anna's cheeks, and she glanced angrily at her sister. Perhaps a secret message was exchanged between the siblings, and then Manek added, 'Only if you can please your teacher with some bribe, you would get some respite from that stringency...'

'Stop bothering the young boy,' said Radhabai as she patted Manek's shoulders. 'This is his first day, and don't bully him!'

Then she turned towards Robi and added, 'Son, don't feel embarrassed. The girls are just trying to tease you.'

Robi turned down his eyes and stared towards his plate and replied obediently, 'Yes, ma'am.'

'I didn't know that boys from Bengal were so shy!' added Radhabai with a motherly grin and overloaded his plate with more food. 'Now, leave behind all apprehension and appease your appetite. A young man like you should be able to eat an entire horse!'

That night went by quietly. It was more of an introductory night, wherein the young man from Bengal was being introduced to the Marathi family of Bombay whose roots were deeply ingrained in British culture.

While heading back to their rooms, Manek whispered to Anna playfully, 'He sure is a beaming and handsome student of yours!'

An embarrassed Anna returned a giggle and went inside her room.

The next morning, Robi came down to the study room, where Anna was waiting for him.

The last night had composed the woman in her. Anna had been able to consolidate herself within the realms of her throbbing heart. She was, after all, the daughter of an acclaimed father, even though her heart felt a wild longing for the vagabond scion of the Tagore family.

In the sprawling study room, she sat in front of the beautiful grand piano as her enchanted student entered the room. Dressed in a well-designed English suit, Robi entered the room, where his supposed teacher was waiting for him.

'Today is our first session,' said Anna. 'So, we shall begin with the etiquette of greetings in the English culture. Then we shall move forward to the manners of table behaviour and eating etiquette.'

Thus began the session while Robi struggled to focus his mind on the teachings by defocusing his heart from the teacher.

As tea got served at noon, they sat down on the sofa while Radhabai served a platter of cookies and cakes.

In the adjacent garden, a man was sweating out in his efforts to nurture the flowerbeds.

'Who is he?' asked Robi as he looked out through the window.

'He is Shantilal, our gardener,' replied Radhabai. 'He has been taking care of our garden for decades. In his dedicated dexterity, he even knows what each of us personally prefers in our garden.'

After another hour, lunch got served, and Dr Atmaram returned with his younger son, Dhyaneshwar. As everyone gathered for their meal, Dr Atmaram introduced his son to Robi. The two were almost of the same age.

'One day, I plan to become a doctor, following in my father's footsteps,' said Dhyaneshwar beamingly. 'Our society needs good doctors so that the countrymen can be provided with proper medical treatments.'

'Robi, or rather Rabindranath Tagore, is ready to set sail for England to pursue a career in becoming a barrister,' commented Dr Atmaram in support of his new guest.

Robi felt speechless. Deep within, he didn't want to follow a stereotyped prescription. However, at that precise moment, he nodded his head and said with a grin, 'Yes…'

The afternoon session was more laid-back while Anna and Robi chatted about each other's likes and preferences. Momentarily, Manek joined them for a quarter of an hour, and the minutes were strewn with funny anecdotes.

'The piano brings in rushes of beautiful and melodious memories,' said Robi. The setting sun was flooding the room with a crimson hue, and Anna sat on a chair in front of him. She had been playing a few pleasant tunes, especially from Western classical music, for Robi.

'My elder brother, Jyotidada, used to play his compositions and I used to sing to him,' said Robi. 'I am an amateur with songs, but I enjoyed creating melodies of my own.'

'Why don't you play something?' she asked. 'I would love to listen to your songs.'

Robi nodded in embarrassment, but she insisted, 'No, please. Do sing something. I really want to listen.'

Thus, he sat in front of the piano and began. It was one of his own compositions. Even though Anna didn't understand the language, she closed her eyes and listened. Her heart soaked in the melody that was unfolding along with the evening.

The sessions went on for days. The ice-wall between the two unknowingly got broken. As Anna taught her handsome pupil, the striking prince in Robi stole away her heart.

One evening, in a fluty, attractive voice, she said, 'Poet, your poetry is indeed beautiful. Can I find a place in them?'

Robi looked at her shyly with a questioning glance, and she stared into his dreamy eyes. Then, she added softly, 'Poet, then give me a special name...'

Robi fumbled as he stood in that strange romantic moment, and then he answered, 'Tomorrow morning, I shall…'

That night was swept in an emotional turmoil, just like the waves of the ocean. Robi left his window open so that the unrestrained winds from the restless ocean could enrich his heart that was seeking an answer.

The next morning, as Robi entered the study room, Anna looked at him, with no tinge of any snobbery, and asked simply, 'So poet, have you found a name for me?'

Robi almost instantaneously replied with a beaming smile, 'Yes... I name you Nalini. The lotus which blooms at the touch of Robi, the Sun!'

It was an audacious statement, but she laughed out loud. That laughter filled his ears like music, and Robi added, 'Nalini is a character from my poetic musings, and I have a poem for her too!'

'Then, dear poet, please recite that ethereal poem to me!' smiled Anna mischievously.

'But these are lines that need to be sung out aloud in the *Bhairavi Raag*, the purest of the ragas! I don't know if I can sing them properly!'

'Robi, I think you must sing!' she replied. 'I will listen to that song before we proceed with our sessions...'

In that bold moment of lyrical fearlessness, Robi sang his poem as his own composed song to her and translated the words for her, while she played the tune on the piano...

Oh! Nalini, open your eyes
Is sleep still to abandon its ply
See standing at your door
The rising sun's first score (Robi—synonym for sun)
Hearing my morning song
See all around, the shroud of sleep has gone
With eyes wringing, the whole world rises
Lusting for a new life
But friend, you sleep, what begets
Am I not your poet...?

Anna listened to his words and then replied softly, 'I think these verses have redefined me today! Perhaps, forever...'

She spun around in an exquisite ballet across the sprawling room, and then she stopped near his shoulder and said softly, 'Poet, I think that even if I were on my deathbed, your songs would call me back to life...'

Her playful encroachment into his life was like the coming of spring! In her mischievous eyes, he discovered an untamed love. His association with Anna was like the natural progression that brought forward a new chapter in his life. A chapter that gave him his first taste of romance in adulthood.

The jovial moments of that romance had the colours of the rainbow. One morning, Robi went out to the garden and met Shantilal, the old gardener. He stood beside the man and asked in a low voice, 'Which is the favourite flower of Annapurna?'

The man returned a sharp, questioning look. Robi felt nervous, and he turned to get back after adding, 'I was just asking. The garden is so beautiful and so nicely maintained. Everyone in the household must be fond of one of the blooms...'

As he walked away a few steps, his heart almost leapt out through his throat as he heard Shantilal's voice, 'Babu...'

Cautiously, he glanced back. Shantilal came up to him and then thrust forth a beautiful red rose into his hand. Then he said with a smirk, 'The little missy loves the red roses! Take it, she will be happy...'

Robi didn't know what to say. Nervously, he hurried away while Shantilal kept on returning short bows and gusts of smirks mingled with each other.

That morning, even before Anna entered the study room, Robi kept the rose upon the piano and stood at the farthest corner. Anna entered the room, saw the rose and picked it up. As her eyes fell upon Robi, the latter shook his shoulders to express his complete oblivion about the existence of the flower.

Anna took it close to her bosom and said, 'Thank you, Poet...'

⁂

The lone monsoon months augmented the solitude of Kadambari. In the household of the stalwart Tagore family, there were many members. Yet, the detachment from her husband, who became busier with the engagements of his own business and his literary endeavours, made her aloof from everyone. Her sisters-in-law were women of substance, and their own aspirations and endeavours made them busy in their isolated worlds. The childhood giggles and gossip vanished unnoticed, and Kadambari became a neglected object within the high walls of the mansion.

On such a monsoon afternoon, as she stretched upon her bed, her mind floated to the vision of a similar afternoon, when her buddy, Robi, was with her...

Sitting near the open window, the two watched the raindrops dance wildly atop the roof. As Kadambari sat and engaged her energies in cutting the betel-nuts into thin, fine pieces, Robi sat behind her and combed her hair.

'Your Jyotidada is so fond of gardens!' she said carelessly. 'He is so busy now with the teething pressure of fine-tuning his work as a playwright and as a businessman taking care of the vast zamindari estate. Why don't we do something to surprise him?'

'*That is a great idea,*' *replied Robi.*

'*In the small open patch of ground behind the Golabari, we can make a secret garden!*' *she said with enthusiasm.*

'*Yes, we would plant your favourite flowers in it...*', *added Robi.*

Her hair fluttered in the moist wind as they giggled happily...

As the flurries of memories swooned away, Kadambari took out the notebook that Robi had left in her custody. She scrambled through the pages, and a smile automatically appeared on her face as she read the amateur lines that he had written years ago.

In a strange desire to be united with her only friend, she took out an empty page in that notebook and scribbled down a few lines of her own...

The smile said, I will be yours forever
But the winds of spring took her away,

The tears said, I will be yours forever
But the towering sorrow forgot her way,

The fear said, I will be yours forever
But the reason for fear forgot how to bother,

The scars said, I will be yours forever
But the ageing heart made them disappear,

The soul said, I will be yours forever
Because I am you, in this life and in the other...

In that solitary moment, she felt content, and she sighed, 'I feel united with your soul. These lines would faint away with the passage of time, but the feeling and the attachment will be perpetual.'

A month had elapsed, and Robi blended into the family of Dr Atmaram. Radhabai, Manek, Dhyaneshwar and Anna were like his own newfound family, where he first tasted the beauty of freedom.

Even Moreshwar, Anna's elder brother, who once visited the family during Robi's stay at Bombay, found him to be a charming lad. He told Robi, 'You must one day visit Baroda. I will personally take you around the town. It is a beautiful place with a serene backdrop. Even though the climate might go to extremes during the summer months, the place has a nostalgia that builds on you. I am sure you will love it.'

One evening, when everyone was busy with their own work, Anna sat beside Robi, after their day's session, and said, 'Robi, let us play an English Game! You must be acquainted with the games of British origin.'

As he sat and listened, she said, 'Think, I am feeling a bit sleepy, so I shall be taking a nap now, while you are free to roam away. However, as per norms, if a man steals away the gloves of a sleeping damsel, then he wins a chance to kiss her!'

Saying those words, she carelessly placed her gloves upon the table beside the sofa and closed her eyes. The moment was too audacious for Robi. He quietly walked up to the sofa, extended his hands and touched the gloves and then picked one up.

Alas, something quivered within his ribcage, and he dropped the gloves upon the table and stood motionless, like a marble statue.

Anna was not asleep. Her heart was throbbing too. However, as the minutes swept away, she opened her eyes and saw a bewildered Robi. With a smile, she touched his cheeks and laughed childishly, 'The Poet is truly an amateur! When will you ever learn...'

The month elapsed, and Robi continued to stay in the household of Dr Atmaram. However, the long detachment from Jorashako made him homesick. When the occasional gathering of rainclouds crowded the sky and the downpours overwhelmed the surface of the earth, Robi's heart felt a pinch of pain as the rush of memories blurred his vision.

One evening, Robi sat in his room and was watching the incessant rain drench the surroundings. The tumultuous waves of the ocean were dancing and splashing upon the beach, and their noise sounded like the echoing laughter across the sprawling veranda of the Tagore Mansion.

Robi looked at the sky and sighed, '*Bouthakrun ... There is so much that I want to tell you. Alas, far away in this distant land, I await a journey across the vast ocean into a land even farther away! A euphoric explosion fills my heart, but this euphoria is different from the joy I relish in your company. Both are different, yet both are so very special. However, this evening, I feel sad as I look at the downpour. My soul wants to speak with you.*'

Drops of tears appeared across the brim of his eyes. Unnoticed, Anna walked into the room. She noticed his melancholy and asked, 'Robi, what happened? Are you missing home?'

'I am missing my best friend. I am missing my childhood companion, who has carved me into the person I am today. I am missing my Bouthakrun...' replied Robi, as he wiped away his tears.

'I have a plan to light up the mood of the Poet,' said Anna cheerfully to ease the atmosphere. 'Now hold one of these,' she said as she picked up a piece of rope. 'I will hold the other end. In the game of tug-of-war, let us see who wins!'

Robi followed her words and held the rope, while Anna held the other end. Then, at the slightest pull on the rope, she rushed in and fell upon his bosom. The lone candle flickered helplessly in the gust of wind through the open window, while the two young hearts palpitated wildly. Anna's face came close to that of Robi, and the eyes met in that wild turmoil. Yet, with a rigid perplexity, the young man stood like stone.

The moments froze and seemed like eternity. Anna stared at him motionless and smiled. Then, she softly moved herself from his body and touched his face with her fingers.

With a fearless sight and a calm face, she said softly, 'Poet, you must never wear a beard. Don't let anything hide the outline of your radiant face.'

Destiny always has a plan. For Robi, it planned a tragedy at the footsteps of every sanctuary of love. So, after two months, he had to sail for England. Thus, in a shattering irony, the unspoken words remained unsaid between the two throbbing hearts.

House of Dr Atmaram. Bombay, Maharashtra. September 1878.

The moment of departure had arrived. Satyendranath was in Bombay, and Robi was all set to sail. The parting day was painful. Tears adorned the eyes of Radhabai, Manek and Anna.

Robi stood like a vagabond, once again, and said his goodbye. It was the day when he was leaving the house of Dr Atmaram to join his Jyotidada.

'Have a safe journey, son,' said Radhabai. 'May all your dreams be fulfilled.'

Saying those words, she quickly went inside to hide away her tears. Dr Atmaram said, 'I wish you all the very best!'

Then, when everyone went inside, Anna came to him and whispered, 'Poet, Robi shall always remain risen in my heart. It shall never set. Every moment will be that new dawn when I, *Nalini*, would blossom.'

'My heart feels a weird earthquake,' replied Robi, like a helpless soul. 'The fleeting time had been too short, and the jolt of destiny is so lethal and ruthless. Anna... I will never forget you!'

'Nalini...' answered Anna. 'From this moment, I am only Nalini, the lotus that blooms in sunlight...in the light of Robi.'

As he walked out through the pathway adjoining the garden, Shantilal stood at a distance with a distraught face. He raised his hand to bid farewell and said, 'The red rose of Missy will await your return...'

Prabashi—A Restless Traveller

'You can't cross the sea merely by standing and staring at the water...'

Separation was never easy, yet separation was his constant companion. Thus, a heartbroken Robi turned his sight away from those melancholic eyes of Anna and moved ahead towards the colossal unknown that his destiny pulled him to. With a strange concoction of emotional turmoil, Robi boarded their ship, named *Puna.* It was the vessel that would take them on their marine voyage. The sight of the endless oceans that had overwhelmed the hearts of greats like Valmiki and Byron, roped in a sentiment of bitterness within him. Hardly did he know what awaited him in the days ahead.

Onboard the ship to Europe.
20 September 1878.

Robi stood atop the rooftop deck of the ship with Satyendranath. Despite being amid a multitude of passengers, his heart felt lonely. Around five o'clock in the evening, the ship started its journey. The two brothers stood speechless as they watched the shores of their Motherland float away from their reach. The crimson hue of the fading sunlight coloured the skyline with enflamed melancholy.

Satyendranath broke the silence and said, 'Robi, the turmoil within the heart is but very common. You are stepping ahead into a voyage towards an unknown land with an unfamiliar culture. However, I assure you that soon you will feel invigorated about your path ahead.'

'Mejodada, I am not sad because I am going far away from my country. I am not worried because I am heading towards the unknown. I am neither sad nor worried. This is a strange emotion that I can, perhaps, never explain to anyone. That never-ending horizon is weeping aloud about the fragility of mortal existence and emotions. The infinite is screaming aloud about the finite nature of a human life! That is brewing up a tornado within me!' replied Robi.

Robi looked at the assemblage of clouds across the sky. Within that coagulation, two faces seemed to emerge within the pupils of his eyes. One was that of Kadambari, his Bouthakrun, and the other was that of Anna, his Nalini.

His voice remained silent, but his heart whispered to him, '*Perhaps, Nalini, I could gather my courage and could speak my heart out aloud... Perhaps, Bouthakrun, I could gather my courage and wipe away your torments...*'

Satyendranath patted his brother on the shoulder, and they smiled at each other. The mammoth ship tore apart the silvery sheath of the ocean and gathered speed gradually. Soon, the outline of land, the contour of India, vanished behind the predominance of the ocean. The ship dwindled and swaggered in its nautical rhythm while Robi went back to the cabin allocated to him. The endless commotion of the excited passengers filled the atmosphere with a strange din while the dwindling motion of the ship created a cacophony within Robi's head. Unable to withstand the strange tumult, Robi locked himself within his cabin that was devoid of even a single open window. Within that encapsulated existence, motion sickness struck quickly and made him break out in a cold sweat. It was a strange experience and it rocked Robi's body, mind and soul.

That evening, the first evening of their voyage, a fellow passenger helped Robi arrive in the dining room and sit at the dinner table. Satyendranath too felt somewhat anxious, but he didn't have the experience or the knowledge to help his brother feel better. The fellow passenger said forcibly, 'Young Mr Tagore, you must eat something or else you will become weaker every day. Seasickness is a very precarious affair. It can make you bedridden for days. However, a lack of nutrition can make you sicker.'

Nonetheless, Robi had already become a slave to the assault of seasickness. Within his head, everything played a ruckus in the euphoric motion of a carousal. His vision had become blurry, and his entire body submitted its strength to the pendulous motion of the ship. He couldn't sit in the dining room for long. Satyendranath and the others helped him to come out, and Robi went and stood along an iron railing across the open deck. In the night, the ship jutted through the mighty ocean with its belching horrific lashes of flames like a monster. The tumultuous ripples became visible in the phosphorescence of the seawater and created a picturesque spectacle.

Alas, the poet within Robi was unable to appreciate that violent beauty. With the help of Satyendranath and the others, he went back to his room and reclined on the bed. Thus, for the next six days, the tall young man was a slave to the torments of the voyage.

'Sir, this is but an unfortunate outcome of seasickness,' said the steward. 'But sir, if you succumb to the assault of this turmoil and devoid yourself of nourishment, then you shall become as weak as a rat!'

The steward of the ship was a man of wisdom, and he had taken a personal liking to Robi. Amid his busy schedule, he always ensured to visit Robi a few times during the day. That afternoon, he sat beside Robi and pleaded, 'Sir, do eat something. Your brother is also very worried about your health. If you don't eat anything, then your health will continue to suffer. I shall do anything to make you fit again. A handsome and kind young man like you must overcome this bout of illness.'

Six days later, as the ship arrived near Aden, the steward came again and said, 'Sir, the sea is calm now. You must get up and come out with me. Let us go to the deck, and you can take in some fresh air.'

Robi obeyed his words and, with his help, came out and sat upon an armchair. The surrounding natural beauty and the gust of fresh air rejuvenated his ailing body. However, Robi was still very weak physically. Satyendranath sat with him, and they gossiped for a while.

Two more days later, the ship arrived at Aden on 28 September 1878. Robi's health showed some improvement, and he felt better. Despite so, he was still very weak. Staring towards the horizon, he felt rejuvenated. The skyline was speckled with beautiful mountain peaks, through whose crevices a beautiful dawn was unfolding. Underneath, the ocean was a facade of tranquillity upon whose bosom numerous colourful sailboats created a picturesque canvas.

Robi took out a piece of paper and began to write…

Dear Bouthakrun,

This time, I shall not break my promise, despite the thrust of seasickness that has broken me down completely. Thus, I am writing this letter to you. As I hold this pen over the piece of paper, my mind seems completely empty, and my heart has become devoid of all emotions. The ocean, which had incited so much romanticism within the hearts of numerous poets, has created such a bitter experience within me. At times, I feel ashamed that such colossal beauty fails to ignite the poet within me. But I am what I am. Perhaps that is what defines me.

Away from home and detached from your affection, I am a restless traveller today. I don't know where this voyage will lead me. However, I shall strive to collect the pebbles of knowledge across the beaches of this wild journey.

My heart writhes for the touch of love, but fate is taking me towards a faraway land. Yes, I had promised you that I shall rise like the 'Rebellious Sun', wherever I am. So, I shall brave through the calamities and come out victorious.

To keep myself engaged, I shall chronicle the details of my escapade and send them to Jyotidada. Perhaps, the novice endeavours of my travelogue would find a place in Bharati.

It is true that most of our beloved attachments often

get torn away from us. Yet, love does touch us in some unknown and wild manner that we can never imagine. I feel detached from your love, but an innocent love did touch me, momentarily though, and I continue to remain a Bedouin in search of my oasis.

Please do take care of yourself. I look forward to that day when I shall once again be united with you and with Jyotidada.

Yours,
Robi

The letter got posted from Aden, and the onward marine journey commenced. However, this time, Robi was fit and fine to experience something radical.

Voyage from Aden to Suez—
Five days across the Red Sea.

Coming out of his shell, Robi stood amid the multitude of passengers on board. They belonged to numerous demographic backgrounds, and their typical natures painted a vivid portrait in his heart, interwoven with joy and pain.

Within the sprawling dining hall, he felt a comical amusement as he witnessed the ladies and the gentlemen. The shy Robi was ever worried about his own conduct amid them and remained cocooned to prevent himself from engaging in any grave misconduct.

Standing beside Satyendranath, he whispered, 'Mejodada, the crowd here is a congregation of such amusing souls. There is no dearth of ladies on board, but the gentlemen are ever grumbling that not one is young or pretty!'

'Well, dear brother,' smiled Satyendranath, 'it is not their fault. Across the entire ship, the ladies, who are past their prime, are struggling to rule over the hearts of the gentlemen with their overburden of forged youthful masks. Whereas, the sole lady who is in the prime of her youthful beauty sits alone, submerged within the pages of the bible, surrounded in her own mystic melancholy, while she shrouds herself away behind her veil.'

The two brothers stared at each other for a momentary pause and then broke out in a hearty laughter. Satyendranath hugged Robi. He felt relieved that his little brother had recovered from his painful suffering.

Amid the gentlemen, Mr B became closely acquainted with them. Courtesy of his benevolent nature, his endless chitchats, his constant laughter and his undying appetite, he established an overwhelming bond with Robi and his Mejodada. By nature, Mr B never deliberated about his own social status or his own age while engaging in hearty laughter with fellow passengers. With a blend of childish innocence and a mature aptitude, he won Robi's heart. With him, young Robi too could engage in pure amusements. By ethnicity, he was Eurasian, but by etiquette, he had mastered the manners of a pruned Englishman.

'Mr Tagore, from now onwards, I shall call you Avatar!' said Mr B with an enthusiastic grin. 'Your tall figure, your intelligent smile and your sober persona merge perfectly into the definition of the name I am giving you! It is my habit, rather, to formulate my own nicknames for the people around me. However, in you, I can see a shine that compels me to call you Avatar!'

Robi smiled shyly while Satyendranath felt amused in their company. Mr B continued his speech while the three of them sat at the dining table: 'For example, look at Mr Gregory, sitting over there, near the corner of this room. I prefer to give him a Hindustani name. Thus, I call him Gor-gori. Ha-ha…'

After finishing a mouthful of food from his plate, Mr B added, 'Look at that gentleman over there. Looking at his physique, I would gladly name him Mr Rohu-Fish! Well. I certainly have my own logical explanation for this nomenclature. With the visible absence of any connection through what we humans know as a neck, his head seems seamlessly joined with his shoulders! Ha-ha … That makes him a perfect candidate for representing the aquatic species!'

Robi was astounded by the humorous knack of Mr B and gobbled his food. After many days of suffering, he felt relieved, and the comical episodes made his heart feel lighter. Within the dining room, amid the diversity of guests, for the first time, he felt somewhat comfortable.

Mr B continued even more vigorously, 'Once a friend of mine was attending an invitation for supper. His companion, an Englishman too, was eating profusely without any hesitation. Looking at him, my friend commented, "Sir, it is true that the food is free and is being paid for by our host, but take heed that your stomach and your gastrointestinal tract belong to none other than you!" Ha-ha…'

Notwithstanding his joke, Mr B forgot about his own monstrous appetite, and Robi smirked at the sight of his colossal famishment.

Amid the passengers, there was a person, named Mr T, who had a gigantic philosophical persona. He always spoke in vintage English, and often his dialogues were like public speeches.

A day later, as the ship was sailing tranquilly, a few young men were engaged in fun and frolic across the open deck under the clear evening sky. Robi, too, was present among them and enjoyed the light-hearted conversation, which was soaked with hearty songs and music. Suddenly, Mr T arrived unnoticed. The extravaganza of the youth got abruptly muted, and they greeted him.

Mr T sat amid them sombrely and then began his philosophical discourse with a heavy pitch: 'Gentlemen, look at the stars above in that beautiful, dark and infinite sky! Have you ever really wondered about the mammoth gorgeousness they harbour? Have you even considered how their fragility and their mysticism are so very comparable with our own fragile human existence? Let me explain to you...'

Thus the thick blanket of philosophical lecture commenced and murdered the youthful amusement of the evening. A few men sat down speechless with gaping mouths, while a few started to yawn! Yet, none dared to intervene while Mr T continued his endless oration. A helpless Robi sat down on a deckchair, stared blankly at Mr T and went into a state of hazy comatose.

Amid the passengers, there was another who attracted Robi's attention due to his peculiar character and behaviour. He had a tall body that could only be compared to an enormous palm tree. With hair like a porcupine's quill, a moustache like that of a massive, untidy broom and a constant frown upon his face. With inexpressive eyes, he engaged throughout the day in bullying the entire staff of the ship!

Meanwhile, during mealtimes, Mr B ensured that he always acquired a place beside Robi. This became his regular habit. Once, during lunch, he looked at Robi and, to his sheer surprise, commented, 'Young man, you are going to Oxford? The Oxford University is indeed a decent educational institution!'

After the arrival in Suez, the subsequent journey towards Alexandria had to be accomplished via the Suez Railway. Being overland travellers, they needed to board the next ship from Alexandria and cross the Mediterranean Sea to reach Italy. From Italy, they had to reach Paris, and from there they were to travel towards London.

Suez to Alexandria to Brindisi to Paris—October 1878.

Robi and Satyendranath arrived in Suez, and the first impression of the foreign land was not very remarkable. With Mr B as their companion, the trio finally reached Alexandria after a long-drawn-out journey by the Suez Railway. The slow and monotonous passage, while being seated inside the dingy compartment of the railway locomotive, not only filled Robi's heart with boredom but also covered his entire body with a thick layer of dust and dirt that floated in unobstructed through the open doors and windows. Even his Mejodada and the other passengers were not spared from this dusty ordeal.

However, the vast stretches of green fields spread across both sides of the railway tracks, the intermittent clusters of date-palm and the lush predominance speckled with occasional sights of human habitation, reassembled the image of Africa that Robi had pictured in his mind ever since his childhood.

At Alexandria, the Mongolia steamer awaited them. This vessel would transport them across the Mediterranean Sea to reach Italy.

On board, Mr B commented with a sigh of relief, 'Avatar, I think we can finally clean off the dust and dirt that have accumulated even within our bones! I am rushing into my cabin. Will meet you soon, once I take a hearty bath. Then we can go for a quick tour of this city!'

Satyendranath too was weary after the long and tiring journey. He added, 'Yes, let us freshen up fast. I am starving!'

Alexandria dazed Robi's heart with her encompassing beauty. The clean stony pathways, the large houses, the predominance of shops and the gigantic Alexandria Port created a sense of awe in Robi. It was a beautiful city, and a tour through the antique getaway lent a refreshing breeze to their weary hearts.

'Do you know that the natives here are multilingual? They can manage to speak in Greek, Italian, French and English. Isn't that wonderful?' commented Mr B.

'Yes,' replied Satyendranath. 'The common language is French, but it is true that most people can speak multiple languages. Look, even the signboards, street names and shop names are written in French.'

The cosmopolitan culture and demography of Alexandria were a very different experience, and Robi soaked in those colourful hues with an open heart.

In the next five days, they sailed across the Mediterranean and reached Brindisi, Italy. It was the first time that Robi set foot upon a European land. In the middle of the icy cold night, they passed the immigration office and finally entered a hotel in Brindisi after another two hours.

Satyendranath looked at a visibly tired yet somewhat excited Robi and said, 'The next train to Paris is at three o'clock tomorrow afternoon. Get some sleep now.'

The next morning, accompanied by Mr B and Satyendranath, Robi boarded a horse-cart for a quick tour around the city. The dilapidated vehicle, the overaged animal and the juvenile driver created a strange and comical contrast.

'*The diver must be fourteen years old, whereas the horse must be fifty! Coupled with their contrast, the cart seems to belong to the prehistoric era!*' wondered Robi and chuckled.

The leisurely city had a laidback atmosphere, which resonated with the residents too. The hustle-bustle of vehicles, the busy movement of officegoers were totally absent, and the people enjoyed a frolic-filled lifestyle.

Sitting upon the primal horse-cart, the trio resonated in the bumpy rhythm while a few kids ran behind them as they screamed aloud in surprise at their skin colours!

'Hooligans!' commented Mr B. 'The unperturbed lifestyle of this city makes them so foolish! Just lend them a deaf ear!'

Then, with an animated gesture of his limbs, Mr B began to weave himself into the role of a tour guide with his heavy baritone: 'Look, there is the ancient church. Behind it is the beautiful floral garden across the playground.'

The seemingly common things that encompassed his speech were ordinary and needed no explanation.

Robi smiled within himself but expressed a vigorous enthusiasm upon his face towards their jovial guest, Mr B, sitting majestically on the horse-cart.

Traversing through the city, they arrived at a huge orchard. The delectable tour among vineyards and apple gardens again crafted a rejuvenated energy in Robi's wayfaring imagination.

A young woman approached him with her bouquet of flowers and a basketful of fruits and said in a soft, melodious voice, 'Sir, would you like to buy something from my collection?'

The exquisite magnificence of the Italian beauty, much similar to the glamour of Indian women, stole Robi's heart. But the young man stood wordless and smiled shyly. Her expressive eyes floated back the glimpse of both Kadambari and Anna, and Robi felt a pang in his heart. It gushed out a strange nostalgia while he fumbled to speak.

At three o'clock in the afternoon, they boarded the train. From Brindisi, the brothers went to Paris. During the course of the lyrical journey, in the lap of Mother Nature, they passed by the famous tunnel of Mont Cenis. It was a magnificent city that was overwhelmingly gorgeous for his taste.

The next alarming experience that Robi had was the visit to the Turkish Bath. Again accompanied by Satyendranath and the ever-adhering Mr B, he entered the subtle structure in Paris. The relentless scrubbing, the scorching steam-chamber of the sauna-bath, the sudden jets of water sprayed from every direction, the heavy massage by the muscular masseur and the swim within the indoor pool were too exhaustive!

'This Turkish Bath is like having one's body laundered by a *dhobi*!' exclaimed Robi.

'Ha-ha... Avatar, all the dust and sand that have accumulated within every pore of our skin, needed this thorough bath to become fresh again!' shrieked Mr B, who seemed to enjoy every bit of the experience.

Then followed a breathtaking tour of the art galleries whose exquisite art exhibitions enthralled the poetic soul of Robi. He whispered to Satyendranath, 'Mejodada, such is the magnanimity of this city and her cultural and artistic heritage that it is impossible to absorb everything in a single day! Perhaps, even a month is not enough to soak in so much of creative genius!'

Arriving in England. Year 1878—

The vibrant portrait of London that was imprinted in Robi's heart was a sharp contrast to the busy city that he witnessed upon arrival. '*Smoky, foggy and wet, with everyone jostling and in a hurry, the image of grandeur is marred by the dull sight in front of me!*' pondered Robi.

The climate and the culture of London were too antagonistic for Robi on his first arrival. A strange sentiment of fear and unfamiliarity gripped his senses. The sensitive soul of the poetic young man, who always dreamt about the vast stretches of English green fields, felt a claustrophobic apprehension. It was cultural shock for the introverted young man.

From London, Robi and Satyendranath reached Brighton. At last, his Mejodada was being reunited with his family while his own tired heart sought the care of a calm home. His poetic acumen felt the fresh breeze of the beautiful English landscape as a renewed inspiration. He felt happy to move in with the family of Satyendranath.

Jnanadanandini welcomed Robi with a warmth of love. 'Robi, I am so glad that you are here. Suren and Indira are super excited and have been waiting for you to come!'

He replied, 'Mejo-Bouthan, I am happy to be here! After the long and tiresome journey across the continents, today I am here in this house that is fragrant with the essence of my family!'

Suren and Indira, aged six and five respectively, rushed in and hugged him. The sudden gust of innocent affection stole away his heart. Robi hugged them back tightly, while drops of tears trickled down from his eyes.

'Why are you crying?' asked Indira softly. In her childish heart, the reason behind his tears was unknown.

'I am happy, so my tears are automatically flowing…' answered Robi with a smile.

'Yes, but people cry when they are sad. If you are happy, then why are you crying?' asked Indira again.

'Maybe someday I will tell you the secret,' said Robi with a smile. 'Even if I am not with you physically, I shall write to you.'

Drenched in the love of two innocent kids, Robi walked into the household of his Mejodada and Mejo-Bouthan. The two young children became his companions who brought to him the images of his own boyhood and the days he used to spend happily with his Bouthakrun.

Yet, Robi had not been sent to England to exchange a home. Thus, he was soon put into a public school. The headmaster of the school, a pruned Englishman, scanned his features and commented sombrely, 'Mr Tagore…what a splendid head you have!'

The nomadic soul of Robi hung around the schoolroom, while a teacher was appointed at home to tutor him. Yet, his nomadic mind hardly found any interest in a formal education. However, in the colourful English backdrop, with his new companions, he absorbed himself to the fullest. With Indira and her brother, despite their minuscule ages, he could open up his heart and speak about the gypsy poet that he was. The English culture and the people he met in England made a deep impact on his heart and mind. It opened up a whole new universe that became a foundation of his future creative genius.

Notwithstanding all the good things, there was something that troubled Robi. It was the English weather. The damp coldness, the severe cover of mist and fog, and the sheer absence of bright sunlight often made him melancholic.

'I just cannot stay in bed till eight o'clock in the morning!' exclaimed Robi one morning.

Jnanadanandini laughed and said, 'The English country would gradually begin to grow into your senses. It is different from India, both in climate and culture. However, I am sure you will soon fall in love with it too.'

One night, in his letter to Kadambari, he poured out his emotions that were bubbling within his bosom.

Dear Bouthakrun,

Life in England is so very different from life at home. Yet, despite all the differences, there are many beauties that fill my heart with joy! When I see little Suren and Indira, their limitless innocence brings in glimpses of my own days at Tagore Mansion. Maybe, in those days, I was like a caged bird who aspired to fly away! Yet, those were the days when I was happy! Yes, I was, because I was with you.

Here, the houses are well kept and clean, the floor well-scrubbed and the furniture shining. Their idea of cleanliness is very different from ours. Thus, personal cleanliness and cleanliness of the surroundings get differential preferences as compared to what I have known ever since my birth.

The absence of the 'Sun' makes your Robi desolate. Thus, the damp coldness hanging constantly in the weather makes my mood dive deep into abysmal depths. However, I try to keep my heart alive with the memories of my early days, and I dive deeper into the depths of poetry to grasp some energy.

Bouthakrun, ever since I left home, I have traversed across our own country and across the oceans to distant lands spread over the continents. I have come in contact with many Gentlemen and have been in the company of many Ladies. Truly, in my deepest feelings, I don't know the reason behind it, but I feel more attracted to dusky Indian beauties compared to the women abroad.

I don't know when, but the day I shall meet you, I will tell you about how my heart has evolved. Some unknown and unexpected strings of this vagabond heart got touched. Yet, they remain solitary, perhaps forever…

I believe that in the course of our life's journey, some angel from a strange and unexpected quarter may cross our path, speaking the language of our own soul, and enlarging the boundaries of the heart's possessions. She comes unbidden, and when at last we call for her, she is no longer there. But as she goes, she leaves on the drab web of our lives a border of embroidered flowers, and forever and ever the night and day are for us enriched.

I shall write no more today. Stay very well, Bouthakrun. Not a moment of mine passes without your thoughts. That sole companion who has sculptured me becomes more and more dear when I am so far away!

Yours,
Robi

The letter perhaps reached Kadambari, or perhaps it didn't. None but Robi knew it. Nevertheless, the emotions etched within those lines reverberated within his heart and led him on the journey towards maturity. Perpetual stability was never destined to be his companion. Thus, as the new life was unfolding in Brighton, Robi's destiny was brewing up some newer plans to be thrust upon him.

Chinna Patra—The Torn Leaf

'We cross infinity with every step.
We meet eternity in every second...'

Life in Brighton. Melinda Villas. Residence of Satyendranath Tagore.
Year 1878–79.

His experience of the English sceneries, the chic ballroom parties, the open-minded women of England, together created a whirlwind within him. However, the stark contrast of the English climate and lifestyle revolted with the life and the Motherland in which his entire existence was immersed.

At Brighton, Robi couldn't absorb the habit of waking up late in the morning. The misty gloom of the morning and the delayed emergence of sunlight to thrust forth daybreak after eight o'clock was too discomforting. Thus, Robi made it a practice to adhere to his basic habits. He started to wake up at six o'clock in the morning. However, his revolt was not limited to it. He used to take a cold shower subsequently!

'Your bravery is beyond comparison!' exclaimed Jnanadanandini, as they sat for breakfast one morning.

'Robi, I wonder how you manage to take these cold showers so early in the morning and still manage to escape from the clutches of pneumonia.'

Robi replied with a smile, 'Due to the years of practice at Jorashako and the blessing of health, which I refer to as a very hard nut, I can miraculously float through those meshes of sickness!'

'Tomorrow evening, we shall attend a ballroom party, and I am sure that you would enjoy it to the fullest! It is a "Fancy Ball". I think you would have fun there,' commented Jnanadanandini.

'Yes, Robi, amid the parties that you have already been to, this "Fancy Ball" would surely be memorable. Dress to your best, and I am sure that the English ladies would be blown over!' smiled Satyendranath.

In his passionate letter to Kadambari, Robi wrote that night, '*Only after coming to this country have I fully realized the worth of our mornings and evenings, and of our moonlit nights!*'

As the moonlight floated in through the glass panes of the window, Robi could see the silvery hue mingle with the thick fog and create a brilliant sight outside. A strange world was unfolding around him. He remembered his own words written to his Bouthakrun from Brindisi in a letter…

> *You are aware of my imaginative nature; I had thought a marvellous sight would open up in front of my eyes as soon as I reached Europe. This must remain in my fantasies and can never be expressed in words. But I have seen since childhood that reality and imagination rarely match. I am unable, due to my nature, to fully experience*

> *many things. Before arriving in a new country, I imagine its newness in such a way that once I am there, it does not seem new anymore; before seeing any grand spectacle, I imagine it to be so grand that in reality it does not seem grand anymore. That Europe did not seem so novel to me made everyone speechless ...*

He contemplated what he had written to Kadambari about his first few experiences of the English ballroom parties: '*I could not bear these ways intended to captivate men—the gestures, the studied lilting tones, the sweet smiles. I don't think anyone can captivate me by these mannerisms and gestures...*'

With a brief pause, he laughed at his own expressions through those words he had written to her. He reclined on the soft bed and sighed, '*I don't know why, Bouthakrun, I try to explain myself and my conduct to you. It is strange. I feel weird when I recall my words. Alas, I cannot stop myself from doing so!*'

Then again, the thoughts about the next evening's party created a lively spark in him. It was a strange contrast that was dancing within his deliberative soul. He closed his eyes and thought, '*What would be different? I don't know. However, I shall be at my best...*'

The next evening, Robi reached the venue of the 'Fancy Ball'. As a custom, every attendee of the party needed to be dressed, or rather disguised, in a decorative manner. Robi went dressed as a Bengali landowner. He wore an exquisite gold-embroidered velvet *jobba*, coupled neatly with a decorative velvet turban. At the request of a few family-friends of Satyendranath, he was made to wear a false beard and a moustache.

One of the English ladies among them commented, 'You look so handsome in it, young man!'

The flattery filled Robi's heart with pride, and he walked into the 'Fancy Ball' with a bosom filled with confidence.

The sprawling ballroom, the exquisite gaslights, the flamboyant music of the band and the congregation of numerous guests roused a sense of awe in his heart. The room was packed with pretty faces, whose radiance was strong enough to diminish the glare of the lights. Wherever he stepped, there were ladies' gowns, and wherever he stared, there was the dazzle of the gaslights. It was like a celebration of beauty, and the overflowing laughter filled the air. The ladies and gentlemen were dancing to the tunes of the music, spinning around deliriously with joy. Despite the cold night that was unfolding outside, the room seemed to be warmed up by the passionate heat in the air.

With awe-filled eyes, Robi saw the men and women dance with each other. The intimacy of their liking for each other was visible in the faces of the couples as they danced through the night, and then the men escorted the ladies to their respective tables that were loaded with delicious spreads of food, fruits and wine.

However, the fake beard and moustache created a problem for Robi. Those with whom he was familiar failed to recognize him. Nobody spoke with him or shook hands with him. A frustrated Robi groaned angrily, '*I must do away with these false embodiments immediately!*'

Then, in a secluded corner, he took off the beard and the moustache and emerged with a wide grin.

'So, how is it?' asked Satyendranath. It had been two

hours since their arrival, and the party was in full swing.

'Some of the gentle ladies, at that corner, have been relentlessly gobbling the food. I am in awe of their appetite!' replied Robi in a low voice and a smile.

Satyendranath laughed while Robi added, 'And I am really surprised to see how much a few ladies can dance! They had been gracing the ballroom with their dance for hours!'

'Mr Tagore, would you like to join me for a dance?' asked Miss A.

Robi was previously familiar with her. He had got acquainted with her at a different event. Her natural beauty, coupled with her kind nature, made him feel comfortable in the foreign culture.

'Of course, madam!' replied Robi with a shy smile, 'I guess I should ask you for a dance with me. Can we do the gallops? I have practised well.'

Thus, with a burst of laughter, Robi danced with Miss A as they did the gallops. Then, with Miss B, with whom he was not familiar, Robi swooshed into a spell of lancers. However, the confused young man committed every possible mistake while engaging in that endeavour.

This was not a singular episode where Robi got an opportunity to socialize with the English. The numerous invitations to various parties earned him vivid experiences. The 'Evening Parties' were another unique experience for him. Dressed in a white shirt, waistcoat, necktie and topped with a prim tailcoat, he attended the evening parties to absorb the subtle behaviour of the English social life.

However, not every episode was very pleasant. There

were moments of embarrassment that created a sense of humour, clubbed with anger.

One night, as Robi sat near the fireplace, Indira and Suren cuddled up near him and asked, 'Tell us something funny.'

Robi recalled an episode that had happened a few days earlier. He said in an animated fashion, 'Two days ago, the Doctor's brother tried to explain to me, in intense detail, about how a camera works and how a photograph is taken! As we walked past a photographer's shop, he pointed towards a photograph on display and began to explain aloud that the camera is such a magical device that can be used to create live photographs and not portraits!'

The children felt amused and giggled, while Robi continued, 'As a mini crowd gathered around me, I tried hard to make him believe that I was well aware of the device! Though it was a humorous episode, I felt relieved about escaping that embarrassing moment, only to arrive at a watch shop, where he again tried to explain to me about how a watch functioned! This was the ultimate...'

The tales were amusing, but they carried a sentiment of divergence that was slowly shaping Robi in the new country. He wrote down many of his experiences in his letters to Kadambari or his brother Jyotirindranath. They had always been his closest confidantes. However, a subtle bond was also getting sculptured between him, Satyendranath and Jnanadanandini.

Jnanadanandini was an educated and strong woman. Her personality had a strong influence on Robi. A few days later, on a bright sunny morning, he went out for a walk with her along the road by the beach.

Robi felt energized and commented, 'Mejo-Bouthan, after many gloomy days and nights, the sun has finally shone up! The warmth of the sunlight really creates sparkles within the heart.'

As they walked, he spoke with her about his experience in England, 'Mejo-Bouthan, here there is a pub on every street corner, but bookshops are rare to find! I feel happy to mingle in the new culture; however, at times, I feel really awkward. At last week's evening party, a Miss asked me if I had seen a piano before! I am amazed by the fact that many people cannot even imagine that the rest of the civilized world is indeed not very different from England...'

Jnanadanandini laughed heartily, but she realized the cultural shock that he was experiencing. Robi added, 'Let me tell you of another instance, Mejo-Bouthan. Consider Dr P, whom my tutor praises heavily as being a highly educated person. A few days ago, when I asked him about Shelley, the gentleman was just aware of his name as a famous poet, but he was completely unaware of Shelley's famous works like the *Cenci* or *Epipsychidion*!'

Jnanadanandini comforted him with her words, 'Robi, the world is different. Every country has its own culture. I am glad that you are able to absorb the shocks and the perks in equal proportions. I am sure, soon this land will enrich your wisdom with the brighter aspects, especially their treatment towards women...'

The words of Jnanadanandini touched his heart. Robi looked at his Mejo-Bouthan and pondered... '*Yes, she is telling the truth. The Inner Quarters of Indian households are like cages! English women are not confined to the house. They converse with friends and at meetings when superior matters are discussed, they listen and may voice their own opinions…'*

His eyes caught a glimpse of Kadambari within the face of Jnanadanandini, and he wondered… '*Bouthakrun, I know, you deserve a taste of this freedom! You are not meant to remain confined…'*

Unfortunately, he could not stay long in Brighton…

Yes, the radical impact on him and his attitude, while he was in England, became a concern. Then, a Mr Palit came up with a brilliant suggestion that got reiterated by Satyendranath. He extended the logic that staying in the proximity of his own family was becoming detrimental for Robi. To make proper use of time and resources, he needed to be away from anything with which he had a familial bond. As per his suggestion, it was decided that he must leave Satyendranath's home in Brighton and stay alone in London.

Satyendranath, as a concerned brother, realized it and said one morning, 'Robi, my brother, if you need to derive any benefit from your education and your life abroad, you should live alone to truly appreciate it. The opulence of parties and the homely warmth among the kids and us would be unfavourable for your proper grooming.'

Robi felt sad. The face of his Mejo-Bouthan became morose while Indira and Suren looked grim. However, as an obedient young brother, Robi nodded his head. Another Bedouin existence was arriving soon in his life.

That night, while sitting inside his own room, he sighed, '*Like a torn leaf, I shall again float away with the winds, to an unknown destination…'*

Lodging House, Regent Park, London.

The onset of winter had already begun its assault. The biting cold pierced through the skin, and the sudden inception of a lonely life, in a faraway land, made Robi desolate without a familiar companion. The trees in the park were devoid of leaves, and the hazy gloom of the mist and the sleet were like the shrouds of death.

An aged butler was appointed at the Lodge to provide the basic necessities of the residents. With a stone-cold face, he supplied the three meals of the day, whose timings were fixed perpetually.

One day, Robi was feeling overly morose as he looked out through the window. As the butler placed the food upon his table, Robi looked at him and asked, 'It seems as if nature is wearing a perpetual frown. The sky is looking so turbid, and the daylight lacks the lustre like a "dead man's eye!" Will it be like this for the entire winter season?'

The butler looked at him with an expressionless face and replied in a monotone voice, 'Sir, in London, winter is white and wet. I don't know what you meant in your question...'

Robi stood speechless for a moment and then said softly, 'It is alright, thank you!'

The arrival in London and the stay at the Lodging House were a very difficult experience. Robi knew nobody around him. To further his educational grooming, a tutor had been appointed to teach him Latin. However, it was a painfully comical experience, once again!

'In each age, one dominant idea is manifested in every human society all over the world, irrespective of there being any outward channel of communication between these different societies! Do you understand the sheer gravity of my research? Mr Tagore, this is revolutionary research!' said the flamboyant Latin teacher.

Robi stared blankly at his tutor. He was absolutely clueless about what was being said. Yet, he understood that it was not a session on learning Latin.

The Latin tutor shook his head sadly and continued, 'I think this subject is very new to your young mind. Let me explain further...'

Robi struggled to absorb his lecture, which was far from being a tutorial session on Latin. In his mind, he could compare the episode with the stringent schooling experiences in Jorashako, where his nomadic mind used to elope with his vagabond soul.

'*He is a good man, but he is somewhat of a crank!*' Robi told his own mind and laughed inaudibly.

Thus, the sessions of pretence continued, and Robi gulped almost a nil dose of Latin that could educate him in his lonely existence.

In contrast, the damp winters created an effect of hibernation within his body, mind and soul. On a cold and damp Sunday morning, he stood by the closed glass window and stared blankly. The wet atmosphere, the gloomy sky and the monotonous drizzle made him feel lethargic. He stared at the lazy raindrops falling languidly upon the windowpanes, and a deep melancholy absorbed him. He lost all his strength and his energy to even write down a letter or do anything creative.

His heart floated away, across the oceans, to his own homeland, to the Tagore Mansion in Jorashako, and then to the fond rooftop room where he used to sit with his Bouthakrun. Monsoon, summer or even winter had very different meanings in that tropical homeland. There was always a delight in the expressions of Mother Nature. Nothing was muted. It was wild like a wild love story, and Robi craved for those moments, soaked in the company of his childhood companion.

As the drizzle gained a little strength and a sleet started to gather, the extreme cold again began to sting across his skin. He wrapped a light shawl around him and closed his eyes.

With a telepathic momentum, his soul got transported to Jorashako, to the room on the roof where he saw Kadambari sitting alone over her bedstead...

'What are you doing here? Aren't you supposed to be in England? How did you reach here?' she asked in a childish awe.

'It is me, Bouthakrun, Robi's soul. My body is still in London, but I have travelled with the winds to meet you. I couldn't stay lonely anymore. I wanted to talk to you,' replied Robi.

Kadambari sat up on the bedstead. Robi looked at the floor, but it seemed like an enormous ocean whose waves rippled near his feet and whose bottom seemed unfathomable. He understood that he wouldn't be able to cross it.

He stared at her face, and she said with a laugh, 'The ocean still separates you from me, but you can stand there and talk to me. Tell me your stories, I am dying to listen to them. I feel so lonely without your mindless chatter and never-ending quarrels!'

Robi smiled and said...

'The cloud, rain, wind, darkness and the cold in London seem perpetual. Even the sound of thunder is so muted.

Here, when the thunderstorms rage through the skies, the cracking noise of the thunder is like the beating drums of heaven! The day begins so late, after eight o'clock in the morning, and ends as quickly as four o'clock in the evening! After that hour, it is so dark that it becomes almost impossible to read anything without a lamp! At times, I wonder if in England it seems difficult to find enough time to work. The night comes riding upon a horse and goes back in a slow walk.

'Now, winter is coming; it is almost at the doorstep. The freezing point has almost been reached at thirty degrees Fahrenheit. Frost has arrived, and the streets have become dry and hard. I was lucky that I had been in the company of Mejodada and Mejo-Bouthan. They themselves and their acquaintances have always helped me adapt to the cultural and social barriers. In their company, I have met many Englishmen and women. My understanding of their treatment of each other has given me a radical worldview. I have attended social parties and ballroom invitations and have had the opportunity to mingle with gorgeous Ladies! However, my heart kept on craving for the dusky beauty of the exquisite women of my own Motherland. None in this foreign land could conquer the heart of this vagabond Bedouin.

'There is so much that I want to tell you, Bouthakrun, about me, my experiences, my sentiments and about the world around me in England. I want to express aloud about the openness in this society that metes out equality among all genders!

'Alas, the wind is gusting. My soul is like a torn leaf. I would have to float back to my body that awaits my return, in London. How will I tell you everything?'

> *'Write to me. I shall eagerly wait for your letter. Your handwriting upon those pages and your fragrance soaked within them would bring me everything that you want to say,' replied Kadambari, with her large eyes on the brink of tears.*
>
> *'Bouthakrun, I promise you. I shall write to you, soon...' said Robi.*

A gust of wind whizzed past, and then Robi opened his eyes. He was still standing by the window, in his room at the Lodging House. He smiled and whispered to himself, '*Yes, Bouthakrun, I promise you, I shall write to you soon.*'

House of Mr Barker, London.

The ordeal at Regent Park didn't continue for much longer. Soon, Robi made arrangements to shift his residence to another place. This time, he became a paying guest in the house of a professional coach named Mr Barker.

On the final day of his Latin tuition, Robi offered to settle his dues. However, the visibly heartbroken tutor replied sadly, 'I cannot accept this payment. I have done nothing and have only wasted your time!'

It was a difficult moment for Robi, but he somehow managed to persuade the man and tried his best to wipe away his remorse with a few kind words.

Finally, he reached the house of Mr Barker. He felt happy to leave behind the dingy, lonely Lodge House and arrive at a new residence. Nonetheless, soon he realized that the new residence was meant to be another rollercoaster ride for him.

Mr Barker was even more odd—though less pathetic—than the Latin tutor. His household comprised him, his docile and mild wife and her pet dog, 'Tiny'. Mr Barker was an extremely gloomy and morose man. The husband and wife seldom exchanged any words or had any conversation. The old man was clumsy in his movements, in harmony with his sombre mood, and kept on bumping into the furniture in the house. Besides the kitchen, he had a dingy room of his own where he spent most of his time.

Mr Barker was, however, hospitable to Robi, especially when he could find some leisure moments after completing his work in the dull study-room that was piled up untidily with books. His wife, too, seemed warm and had a motherly affection. The couple was childless, and she was a harmless creature who was trying to cope with her pathetic life. Mr Barker welcomed him in an energetic but heavy voice, 'I welcome you to our household. I hope that your stay will be comfortable here. Please pardon me if my wife's favourite dog causes any trouble. I will try to do my best so that he doesn't…'

The days moved on, and Robi observed the weird, silent battle that perpetually ensued between the couple. He felt awkward remaining amid them. It was like the existence of a goldfish inside a glass bowl, whose owners were in a cold war with each other!

The gatherings within the house, especially during meals, were the most awkward. They sat silent and glum through the dinner, much to the discomfort of their young guest. Yet, the hosts remained unperturbed.

One evening, as they sat for dinner, Mr Barker wanted a second helping of the potatoes. He mumbled shoddily, 'Some potatoes...' (the word 'please' remained inaudible).

Mrs Barker mumbled back, 'I wish you were a little more polite.'

Mr Barker protested, 'But I did say "please"!'

'I did not hear it,' said Mrs Barker.

'It was no fault of mine!' remonstrated Mr Barker.

Then, a gripping silence befell the entire dining room. Robi looked in every possible direction to sweep away the grim atmosphere. However, as he failed in his endeavours, he gobbled up his food and went back to his room after wishing them a polite goodnight.

The friction between them was more than what was visible. One day, Mrs Barker was playing the piano to Robi when Mr Barker barged in with a grumpy face, 'When are you going to stop?'

Mrs Barker replied crossly with a surprised face, 'I thought you had gone out!'

The musical session got terminated that day, and thereafter, whenever Robi requested Mrs Barker to play something on the piano, she whispered, 'I will play the piano for you when that horrible man is not at home!'

Amid that sombre setting and the grey ambience, Mr Barker tried his best to sit with Robi in the sitting-room and chat with him. The conversations often were intended to be lighthearted, but Robi found it difficult to absorb the dark vibes. Then, to add to the grimness, Mr Barker ensured that he tortured the poor dog, 'Tiny', when he wanted to punish his wife!

In the distant land, amid weird people, Robi began to feel claustrophobic. He poured out his heart in the pages of numerous letters he wrote...some for his

Bouthakrun (as per his promise) and some for his Jyotidada.

And then, the letter from Jnanadanandini arrived, as a wind of spring...

She had written...

Dear Robi,

Your Mejodada has taken a cottage in the picturesque Torquay. Devonshire is a beautiful seaside resort town. We are spending the spring season in that cottage. We really want you to join us. Even the children, especially Indira and Suren, are eagerly waiting to meet you. Please come immediately, and we can travel together...

The letter was like a detonator to a bomb of oxygen within him, and he exploded with limitless joy. Robi packed his belongings and bid a hasty farewell to Mr and Mrs Barker and fled at top speed to be united with the only family he had in England.

Torquay, Devonshire. Spring of 1879.

The attractive coastline on the English Channel was popular for beaches, such as Babbacombe and Cliffside Oddicombe. Torquay Harbour near the town centre boasted numerous shops, cafes and a marina. Torre Abbey, an age-old monastery, had art galleries and extensive gardens featuring exquisite plants. In totality, the beauty of the getaway was truly breathtaking. In the open country and amid the company of the children, Robi felt relieved, once more. Spring was unfolding everywhere, and the beaches were becoming more and more occupied by the rush of people.

One sunny morning, as they went out for a walk along the marina, Robi sat on a wooden bench beside Satyendranath and Jnanadanandini, and said, 'Devonshire is so attractive, yet it has failed to sprout a fountain of poetry within my poetic soul…'

'Robi, the poet always needs to be with his muse!' replied Jnanadanandini. Satyendranath smiled at his wife's witty response. She continued, 'Amid the unfolding beauty of Springtime and in these boundless rocky beaches, you must search for her. I am sure, when you meet the muse of your inner soul, you will also notice the fountain. It would automatically reincarnate the poet within you!'

Her words touched him. The next morning, with a fresh mind, he ventured out across the coast to fulfil his poet's destiny. Walking by the bay, he reached atop a mound. There, he selected a lonely spot on a rock overhanging the sea. Quietly, he sat down upon it and took out a notebook and a pencil.

He closed his eyes while the saline sea-breeze fluttered his hair. Then he opened his eyes, and with a smile on his lips, he wrote down *Bhagnatari (The Broken Boat)*. The hours floated away and germinated the inception of a wonderful and heart-wrenching verse…

The pretty locales of Devonshire, coupled with the beautiful moments spent in the company of the children, Satyendranath and Jnanadanandini, were like a refreshing break for him. The days spent in the company of various other people—Dr M, who was ever willing to teach his acquaintances about Christianity and the gospels, the ladies at the ballroom parties, Miss K who was surprised by his naivetés on not knowing how to even identify a bride among a crowd in a wedding party—enriched him to be aware and be critical about the social diversities. Yet, he learnt much and began to appreciate those diversities too. It was a pleasant metamorphosis.

As the days went by, he returned to London and joined the London University, where he attended Henry Morley's lectures on English literature. He read with him *Religio Medici* and some plays of Shakespeare, and was much impressed with the professor's wonderful way of teaching.

Back in London, luck favoured him in a positive way, and he finally managed to get accommodation in the house of one Dr Scott.

House of Dr Scott, London. Year of 1879.

So, the turn of destiny took him to the household of Dr Scott, away from all things that could distract his mind. Amid a foreign culture, a hurricane was again about to make landfall.

The white-haired and well-mannered Dr Scott was welcoming in his approach. As Robi arrived at their residence, Dr Scott greeted him and said, 'I am sure you will have a pleasant stay in our house. We are a calm and happy family. At present, with me are my wife and my eldest daughter. My two younger daughters are not present now. They are at a relative's residence for a few days.'

Robi smiled in response, but his eyes caught the glint of playful mischief in the eyes of the doctor's eldest daughter. Mrs Scott had a motherly affection that greeted him with warmth.

Suddenly, the pet dog came rushing in to inspect the newcomer, and Robi froze like a statue for a few moments. Dr Scott asked the housemaid to take the dog away and said, 'This was Tabby, our pet. Don't bother, he is a friendly fellow and would soon become acquainted with you!'

As he reached up to his room, the housemaid brought in his luggage, and while leaving, she whispered to him, 'The younger girls are afraid of you. They think a dark invader, a "blackie", from India, is raiding the house. So they have run away in alarm!'

Robi handed over a coin to her, which she received with an overjoyed grin, and then he replied, 'Soon everyone will know that I am as harmless as a butterfly!'

Indeed, with a buttery smoothness, Robi mingled within the household. Dr Scott, Mrs Scott and their eldest daughter found him to be a charming man who had an attractive persona. Even Tabby, the dog, became fond of the tall young man from India and soon acquired a habit of playing with him heartily before each of his major meals. Without a playful session with Robi, he refused to even eat his meals at times.

A few days later, Robi sat across the fireplace and said, 'I am already enrolled in the University of London, but I am struggling with what I am learning. Alternatively, English literature attracts my romanticism. Inside my heart, I am a poet.'

Mrs Scott listened to him and firmed up a plan in her mind. Thus, every evening, she made him sit at the wooden table by the fireplace and recite varied literary works from which he was able to seep the sweet honey of literary passion.

He expressed his happiness to Dr Scott and said, 'At last, in London, I don't feel lonely. Far away from home and from my own people, in this house, I get the warmth of a family that I can feel as my own.'

Dr Scott replied, 'Your manners and your words are so very refined and touching. It makes me believe that you have been part of this family for ages!'

Within ten days, Robi had become an integral part of the family. Every day while returning from his classes, he fetched two bunches of roses, one for Mrs Scott and one for her eldest daughter.

Mrs Scott said with a laugh one day, 'Robi, I hope I am pronouncing the name correctly, I feel flattered by the love that you have shown for us. Dr Scott would have been very jealous if you were not like a son to me!'

That afternoon, as the housemaid came to clean Robi's room, he took out a bunch of lilies and gave them to her. The lady stood spellbound while he said, 'I am really thankful for everything you do for me! This is my expression of saying thank you!'

She stood speechless for a few moments and then whispered with a giggle, 'The younger girls are coming over the weekend. They are assured that you are harmless ...like a butterfly!'

Then, a few days later, on the weekend, the two younger daughters of Dr Scott arrived. The tall and handsome guest was a man who instantaneously drew them with magnetic attraction. However, the winds of taboo prohibited a direct confrontation.

Lucy Scott, the third daughter of Dr Scott, looked into the eyes of the tall, handsome young Robi and her heart got swept away! As the ice broke between the girls and Robi, Lucy sat in the sitting-room, in front of the piano beside the fireplace, and asked with a soft voice, 'Do you like music? I love singing. English and Irish songs are my favourites.'

Presently, a strange struggle commenced wherein Miss A, the sister of Lucy, too got attracted towards him! It was a tussle of elusive romance in the liberal family of Dr Scott, and Robi became the heartthrob in the triangular tale of love.

Robi felt a pang of Cupid in his heart. He was eighteen years old, and the onset of early youth created flutters within his stomach as he sat in front of the dreamy yet beautiful Lucy. Miss A was perhaps physically more attractive, but the nomadic soul of Robi found peace in the eyes of Lucy.

The family of Dr Scott carved a different persona inside him. He started to appreciate the beauty within an English household. He began to grasp the wonderful freedom that women could enjoy in England.

The friendship with Lucy grew quickly and passionately. Unlike his association with Anna, while he was in India, this relationship blossomed boundlessly.

'The green leaves of plants and colourful petals of flowers create a romantic joy within me!' said Robi to Lucy on a bright Sunday morning.

Lucy smiled in reply and said, 'Then we must plant some saplings. With love and care, they would soon become beautiful.'

'Teach me to sing your English and Irish songs,'

demanded Robi. 'And I shall teach you to speak in Bengali.'

A fond smile came upon her face, and she nodded her head in agreement, 'Yes, I will. And you must teach me to also sing in Bengali, especially your poems!'

Robi felt happy in the passionate moments. During his stay in Devonshire, he had been in the company of several ladies who were interested in him. There was a Miss M, particularly, who courted him desperately while she brooded upon the classics of Western music. However, Robi had never felt the urge to reciprocate those courtships. He always shied away from them, even though he enjoyed the warmth of attractive feminine company.

But the moments when Lucy sat with him in the garden and planted the saplings, and their fingers touched each other carelessly, Robi felt like singing aloud a song of romance.

Far away from the fences of the orthodox society and the stalwart 'Tagore' family, he experienced the boundlessness of love. He played muse for the beautiful girls of Dr Scott, in whose eyes he was a Casanova. In the flirtatious moments, they felt playfully joyous in his company. Yet, Lucy became special with each passing day. While a strange attraction drew him towards the other daughter as well, Robi held back his vagabond heart from getting lost. The romance made him a nomadic traveller who was destined to become the famed bard. He was, by nature, fearful of women. But this time he didn't try to keep a distance. The blizzard of youthful encroachment of romance was too hard to resist.

With the family of Dr Scott, especially the two

daughters who doted on him and more so with Lucy, the attachment became stronger with every passing day. Miss A was passionately crazy about him, but soon she understood the vibes in his heart. She refrained from aggressively seeking his company. Nevertheless, her love for Robi never diminished. Within her heart, the Rebellious Sun created the warmth of a springtime day, maybe perpetually.

On afternoons, Lucy and Robi would sit together and sing. On evenings when the sky became gloomy with clouds, they sat together and recited poems of romance. On many such evenings, Robi joined the girls in a table-turning séance. On the first day, as they began the game, Lucy explained the rules to Robi, while her sister returned a frown.

Lucy mentioned, 'We would place our fingers on the tea-table, and it would go capering about the room. It got to be so that whatever we touch begins to quake and quiver.'

Mrs Scott was not very fond of the game, but Robi felt excited about engaging in this adventurous plan. Mrs Scott gravely shook her head and said, 'I have my doubts about this being right!'

Yet, she didn't resist as she didn't wish to dampen the spirit of the game. This strange game continued for a couple of days and it mingled with bouts of laughter and chivalrous joy. However, one day, when they chose to put their hands upon Dr Scott's top hat to make it turn, Mrs Scott rushed up in an agitated state and forbade the progress of the amusements. Thus, the strange game came to an end, but the spring in the hearts of the youthful souls continued to bloom.

A few days later, one solitary evening, Lucy held his hands in a passionate moment and said, 'I hope that time would freeze. I wish that this moment would never pass... Robi, I really hope that the sun would never set and this day would never die!'

'The Rebellious Sun is lucky today,' replied Robi. 'Perhaps fate would be kind enough to grant your wish...'

The stark contrast of the lifestyle in London, especially the openness that the ladies were able to enjoy, continued to create turmoil in his heart. In his letters to his family, especially to his beloved Bouthakrun, Robi started to frankly compare the orthodox culture back home with the free-minded and fresh behaviour seen in the Western world. The distinction between the outer quarters and the inner quarters, specifically designed for the men and the women respectively, was something that he started to question.

In a strong letter that he wrote within his diary and later posted back home, to his family, Robi expressed the contrast in familial culture that he experienced in the house of Dr Scott...

> *We do not give the name of servitude to slavery within the family, but we can, at the most, gild it with a name and transform the iron fetters of discipline into those of gold, but cannot erase its restrictions—the harmful effects persist. I had once thought that Hindus were by nature simple and spontaneous, without any unnatural restrictive laws. But I am ashamed to say that any more. Hindus without unnatural laws? Just peep into their families! Just look at the rigidity between brothers and*

sisters, mother and father, men and women... It is even forbidden for one to talk too much or even laugh in front of one's elders. How terrible! If you cannot talk freely to those with whom you spend twenty-four hours of the day, cannot laugh heartily, if in their presence you have to rein in your tongue, place a weight on your happy countenance and wear a mask of reverence the livelong day, where then do you go for your relaxation?

English homes have a feeling of cheerful relaxation. Parents, brothers and sisters, wives and sons gather around the fireplace and cheer it up with their happy talk, laughter and singing. After a hard day's work, one returns home to a sense of joy and familiarity. In my beloved home, in one room, the father-in-law, along with his clutch of elderly friends, sits drawing on the hookah and blames today's generation and its unholy behaviour for the impending onset of divine recrimination. In another room sits the bride of the house, her veil drawn over her face, silently listening to her mother-in-law ladling out her daily dose of blame. In another room, her husband, along with his young friends, gossip maliciously—no one in England could imagine such a scenario.

In our families, we have to make strangers our own, because our own are strangers to us.

The young girls of Dr Scott became more and more infatuated with his handsome persona and masculinity. The affection of Mrs Scott was overwhelming and carved a respect for feminine power in him. Robi was in the centre of a romantic upheaval.

The association was beautiful, and he continued to

write letters, openly praising the freedom and movement of Western women. In another letter, Robi wrote with a fierce valour, as if the Rebellious Sun had once again risen in the *West* to speak his heart out! Perhaps those were his words for the women in his own family. Perhaps those were words that remained unspoken within him to protest against the sadness of his Bouthakrun...

> *The English women are not confined to the house; they converse with friends and at meetings when superior matters are discussed. They listen and may voice their own opinions. In the presence of people, a very happy and pleased expression is presented. Although she herself may not be a witty person, she enjoys a good joke, is generous with her praise if there is something she likes, and laughs heartily if she hears something amusing. It is not ideal behaviour for women here to keep their lips sealed or to be overcome with shyness... A bit of reticence is not unpleasing to the eye, one may even see some poetic sweetness in it—but to deal with shyness the livelong day is painful indeed.*
>
> *If one is rewarded with an answer to one's question after two or three hours of perseverance, one can bear it once, but if one is brought to the brink of exhaustion each day in trying to get her to say a few words, it would then be difficult to survive. If you cannot share a joke with me without inhibition, I would be forced to dissociate myself from you and look for other company. The 'mantras' chanted at the wedding ceremony will not magically give rise to love. Marriage by itself does not lead to love. If no love exists between my wife and me, and if my wife cannot keep me entertained with lively*

conversation, will I not look for sources of amusement elsewhere, leaving my mute lady companion behind...?

At Jorashako, the rebellious letters were received with a huge shock. Dwijendranath Tagore was speechless at the audacious and open expression of his young brother.

He stood in front of the entire family and exclaimed, 'Women can never share with men the kind of conversation they have with friends of the same sex in the inner recesses of the house. The presence of a man in their midst would only mar their enjoyment! I am alarmed by the statements that Robi has made. The impact of the West is too vivid and outrageous in his self.'

As the matter created ripples within the family, his father, Debendranath, got alarmed and decided to call him back immediately.

None noticed, but standing quietly at a corner, Kadambari smiled a silent smile. A glint of joy sparkled across the pupils of her eyes. She had spent so many seasons without the only companion she had in the sprawling Tagore Mansion.

Inside her room, where she was ever lonely, devoid of the company of her husband too, she opened the old notebook and wrote down a few lines of her own that were bleeding from her heart...

The chills of winter bit across the dry skin,
The limping heart was bleeding out thin,
The scent of Spring would soon be gone,
The blossom of romance was so very lone,

The scorching heat of Summer was fuming,
The burnt heat of passion was like a musing,
The winds of Autumn taught him to let go,
A touch of love was like a fire on the snow,
Sometimes, letting go is the best,
So that, in peace, can the lone soul rest…

The bright days at the house of Dr Scott were thus abruptly cut short in three months…

The news from Jorashako reached Satyendranath, and it was communicated by him to Robi. Satyendranath wrote to him, 'Baba wishes that you return to India immediately. Along with me, Jnanadanandini and the kids, you would have to travel back.'

The day of parting arrived soon. Lucy was heartbroken. Her tears erupted profusely and then dried within her heart. She held Robi's hands and said, 'Fate has not been kind enough, Rebellious Sun...'

Mrs Scott had found a subtle affection towards this young boy. She embraced him lovingly and said, 'Why did you come to us, if you must go so soon...'

Robi held her hand, looked at her daughters and then his eyes came and halted upon Lucy. With tears trickling down from his own eyes, he replied, 'Forget me not... I promise I shall come to you again. The unconditional love I have got would never let me be far away...'

A heartbroken Robi was thus left a failure in achieving what his father desired him to be. Like a torn leaf, once again, he returned to India in February 1880.

The few months he spent with the family of Dr Scott and the moments of a budding romance with Lucy left a lasting impression on his heart.

As the ship floated deep inside the endless ocean, Robi stood alone upon the deck, watching the setting sun beyond the horizon and wondered, '*The Rebellious Sun too is setting. Yet, he shall arise in another morning. In the crimson rays of that new dawn, I shall create my poetry. In the lines of those verses, the touch of love that has bewitched me will remain immortal...*'

Kari O Komal
The Sharps and the Flats

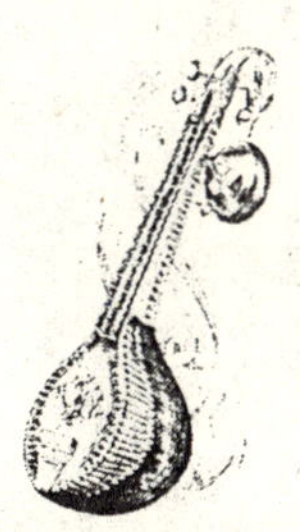

Vivah—The Misunderstood Union

'I slept and dreamt that life was joy. I awoke and saw that life was service. I acted and beheld…service was joy…'

Robi stood at the entrance of the moderately English-style bungalow. Situated at a little distance from the Bombay beach, it looked serenely beautiful. It was a familiar and prized sight, and he couldn't believe his own eyes. The small, vibrant garden still oozed the beauty of colours through its withered blossoms. Yes, he was standing outside the bungalow of Dr Atmaram.

Old Shantilal looked a bit older and timeworn while he sat near the lone rose bush in that little garden. It was the sole bush whose blooms had not withered. In Shantilal's eyes, he could read the silent words, 'The red roses for Missy have awaited your return… I have kept my promise. Now it is your turn…'

There was a strange mist that surrounded the entire place, making it seem isolated from the rest of the world. In his eyes, it seemed like heaven. A mystified Robi looked around, searching for a much-desired sight.

Then, like magic, from within the mist, the door of the bungalow opened, and she came out. Yes, it was her, yet her eyes were lost in a dreamy halo, and they didn't get a glimpse of the visitor.

Robi extended his hands beyond the unnecessary fence of foliage that was born from the dry branches, and said softly, 'Anna…'

Her trance broke as his voice echoed in her ears while his fingers touched her. She looked at him as a soft smile bloomed upon her face. She replied, 'No… I am Nalini.'

Robi's heart swelled with delight, and he was about to utter something when she whispered, 'Could you really come? Robi, could you really break through the glass door? Or, is it a fantasy?'

Within a moment, the distance of an ocean floated in, and she went away from within his reach. A perplexed Robi looked at Shantilal. The latter laughed sardonically and added, 'The red roses for Missy would await your return…'

As a gush of perspiration crowded across his forehead, Robi saw the frame of Anna slowly getting disintegrated into a tempest of rose petals that swarmed around him and then melted within a bright aura. His heart screamed out aloud, 'No, Nalini…!'

Then, within that halo, a new face emerged. It was the face of a little girl. It was the face of Indira…

Robi got up hurriedly, as he realized that he had dozed off while he was reclining upon the deck chair of their ship. Indira stared at him and asked, 'Were you dreaming? What were you dreaming about?'

'Yes, I was dreaming. But I hope it was not a dream,' sighed Robi. Then he looked at the confused face of his niece and said with a smile, 'One day, I will write to you about the dream and everything you ever wanted to know from me. I promise...'

Indira smiled back and added, 'We have almost reached Bombay. Come inside quickly.'

In Bombay, did he attempt to fulfil that unfinished dream? Did he try to go back to the bungalow and meet his Nalini? The intrigue and mystery remained deeply conserved within him.

~

Year 1880. Tagore Mansion. Jorashako, Bengal.

'So, you have come back,' said Kadambari as he stood in front of her. 'What should I call you now? Robi or Rabindranath the Englishman? What is it that you have brought with you after almost two long years?'

The contempt in her words pierced his heart. She was hurt. She was perhaps lonely. Nonetheless, her words jutted out like arrows to imprison him, whom she possessed.

'Bouthakrun, I have returned empty-handed,' he replied. 'I only have memories, just memories. And I have my unfinished memoir of those memories that I have fondly named *Bhagna Hriday*, the broken heart.'

His words ceased as he stood quietly. She opened her cupboard, took something out and came up to him. She handed over his notebook. Then she touched his fingers and said, 'Take this; it is your notebook. Remember, you have not come back empty-handed. My Rebellious Sun has matured into a wonderful new dawn. Take this and create your magic...'

A sudden ecstasy filled his heart as he held the notebook. He replied with a smile, 'Yes, I will.'

As he walked down the stairs and passed through the corridor, he overheard the sweeper and a few servants gossiping inside a shady corner. While the others listened, one of them commented, 'Robi Baba has returned without any academic degree or distinction. In seventeen months, he has garnered no merit for himself or the family.'

'How do you know so much?' asked one of the servants.

The former replied, 'I have overheard the elders of the family. They think that he is a man of no merit. He has wasted his time in a foreign land, and that is why the Maharshi had summoned him back. What a waste...'

Unknowingly, two drops of tears surfaced near the brink of Robi's eyes. As the evening breeze fluttered his hair, he wiped away those teardrops and went back. However, the murmur didn't refrain.

Thus, in the eyes and words of uncles, aunts and distant cousins, who visited the Tagore Mansion, the mockery remained afloat: 'Robi, how were the days in England? Too bad that you couldn't complete your studies. Well, there is always a chance to start afresh...'

Despite every contempt, Robi became more carefree and happier. He was happy to be back home, and he immersed himself in literary creativity. He poured himself out in a cascade of songs and wrote his first musical play, *Valmiki Pratibha*. The prime significance of the play remained in the fact that it was his first musical innovation, where his revolt against the prevailing orthodox tradition in Indian music was shattered by his own harmonious concoction of Western Classical and Indian music!

It was a time when, within the Tagore Mansion, a cascade of musical emotions was gushing forth day after day. Within the scattered and nomadic sprays of that cascade, a rainbow got born in everyone's heart. The champion of that sonata was the broken heart, the untamed beast... Robi. His tragedy and his elation created a supreme harmony that broke all barriers.

As he finished his work on *Valmiki Pratibha,* he told Jyotirindranath and Kadambari, 'Jyotidada, Bouthakrun ...this is not a play to be read. It is a play to be heard and seen!'

'Excellent idea,' replied Jyotirindranath. 'Robi, you must arrange to enact this performance within our Tagore Mansion. Members of the family, friends, relatives and neighbours would be invited to witness the performance.'

So, *Valmiki Pratibha* was much encouraged by its stage success as it got enacted on the terrace of Tagore Mansion. He himself took the role of Valmiki while his niece, Pratibha, played the character of the little girl whom the dacoits had abducted and whose innocence metamorphosed the chief, Valmiki. However, something even more complicated was slowly unfolding around him. It was a success that augmented his confidence manifold.

Dressed in apt costumes, little Pratibha performed as the incarnate of Goddess Lakshmi. She looked at Robi, her vagabond protector in the play. Under the flames of the torches, surrounded by the darkness of the night, the audience in the Tagore Mansion of Jorashako watched their enactment and remained enthralled.

The little goddess gifted Valmiki with the gift of music and said in a musical expression, '*The music of pity which melted your stony heart shall become in your heart the music of humanity softening and chastening millions of hearts. Your voice shall resound from land to land, and many poets would echo your songs.'*

A speechless murmur of appreciation filled the air on the terrace. Maybe it was a true blessing in disguise that touched the bard in that musical moment that he had himself created.

That night, as he reclined upon his bed and looked out through the open window, the twinkling stars smiled at him from the clear dark sky.

Robi smiled back at them and said, 'Maybe I have not come back as a scholar, but I have gained much. Travel has not only made me richer but also made me feel the depths of love. Tonight, under the canvas of the dark night in the presence of the stars that are so very alive, I wish... I will be able to retain the love that I have been blessed with. I wish...this broken heart would gather the courage to scream out aloud and express its love for you! Yes, the love for you, Anna! Yes, the love for you, Lucy! Painted in my verses, I will tell the whole world that I had indeed fallen in love!'

As Jnanadanandini, the rebellious lady of the Tagore Mansion, strode on to break down the chains of age-old restrictions on women in the house, in her praises for Robi, she gradually came closer to him. Her sudden eavesdropping into his life, with a motherly affection, made a wound in another heart that was always protective of Robi. Thus, soon, a new episode started to unfold within the inner quarters of the Tagore Mansion. As Robi immersed himself in the elevated zeal to create literary designs, his Mejo-Bouthan became a constant admirer of his literary genius.

One evening, as Robi sat upon a couch and focused

his energies on another play, *Kaal Mrigaya* (The fateful Hunt), Kadambari sat at a distance. Presently, Robi looked at her and said, 'Bouthakrun, listen to these few lines and the surreal tune I have imbued them with...'

As he orated the lines in his own composed tune, Kadambari exerted her usual criticism and replied, 'This is very ordinary. I don't find an excellence that would remain perpetual...'

Robi felt cross. His efforts had just been marred by her comment. He held the notebook in his hand and silently protested. However, the melodrama got cut short as Jnanadanandini entered the room and suddenly snatched away the notebook from his hands.

At first, Robi tried to protest, but in vain. Jnanadanandini read a few lines and then said enthusiastically, 'Robi, I want to listen to these few lines. They are very intriguing.'

A vengeful Robi took a glance at Kadambari and then orated the paragraph in his composed tune. As he finished, Jnanadanandini said aloud, 'This is so beautifully done. I can feel the fantastic blend of the Western and the Indian melodies. Robi, you must develop this further.'

The appreciation made him feel confident. Yet, to irritate Kadambari perhaps, he replied, 'Mejo-Bouthan, you can keep the notebook tonight if you wish to read the verses. Meanwhile, I will work on the melodies.'

As Jnanadanandini took it happily, Robi added with an elevated voice, 'Mejo-Bouthan, your appreciation gives me confidence.'

The silent cold war lasted a few days, and soon, *Kaal Mrigaya* was ready to be enacted.

A few days later, it was performed on the terrace of Tagore Mansion, amid a captivated audience. Robi undertook the execution of the play, and he himself acted in the role of the blind hermit. The theme of the work was based on the ancient legend of *Ramayana.* It too received great appreciation.

The thirsty soul of Robi sighed into his ears, '*I hope the arrows of failure would be wiped away by the vibes of literary music.*'

However, a richer harvest lay ahead, awaiting the heat of the Rebellious Sun, to ripen it. For that heat to emanate, destiny showered another shock on him.

One morning, as Robi loitered around the terrace garden, Kadambari came up to him and said, 'Your Jyotidada and I are leaving the city for a long sojourn. We would travel in three days.'

The suddenness of the news left him speechless for a few moments. Then he revolted, 'This is not fair! How can you abandon me when I have come back to you?'

'Did I ask you questions when you left?' replied Kadambari in a mild rebellion. With her eyes looking elsewhere, she added, 'Robi, you were away for seventeen months. You were becoming richer with your travels, and you were making new acquaintances, while I sat and waited. Separation is an inherent part of life. Face it now.'

Robi looked at her blankly while she opened her cupboard, took out something and came up to him. She placed a notebook in his hands and continued, 'Before you went away, you had kept your notebook in my custody. I protected it and returned it to you. Now, when I am leaving, I give you this. It is my notebook. Her pages contain pieces from my heart. I am no poet;

these are my simple expressions. I don't want to keep it in your custody. Robi, I want to give it to you. Read it when you can and when you want.'

Robi took it obediently. Kadambari smiled and added, 'Promise me, you will read it alone. These words are not for the world to know. If ever I am not there, promise me that you will destroy this. That would make my memories eternal...'

He nodded his head and said softly, 'Yes, I promise.'

As he came out and went inside his own room, a strange emotion erupted within Robi. He kept the notebook upon the wooden desk, while the wind fluttered its pages.

His eyes fell upon one of the pages, and he saw what was written…

In a moment, a smile cries
In a moment, a hope dies,

In a moment, a dream awakes
In a moment, a heart breaks,

In a moment, faith becomes a stranger
In a moment, love can breathe no longer,

In a moment, a storm is born
In a moment, all memories are worn,

In a moment, daylight can shine
In a moment, truth turns out divine,

In a moment, a foe can be a friend
In a moment, a life comes to an end,

In a moment, the universe is … In a moment.

The day of departure arrived soon, and Jyotirindranath and Kadambari bid their goodbyes. Jyotirindranath gave Robi a confident hug and said, 'My little brother, keep churning out your creative excellence. *Bharati* would be a proud representative of your works. I am so very happy about you.'

As Kadambari and Jyotirindranath boarded the carriage, Robi stood at the veranda of the inner chambers, near a corner. In that moment of separation, a sight again flashed passed Robi's eyes...

A little girl dressed in a traditional wedding saree walked upon the marble floor with her soft and naive footsteps, as she shyly tried to hide her face behind the half-drawn veil. Maybe she noticed the little boy standing afar, or maybe she didn't; nobody knew. For a moment, she halted and lifted her eyes from behind her veil.

It was a reminiscence of the day, many years ago, when he had embarked upon a journey with his father to the Himalayas, while she stood alone at the same corner. Soon, the carriage went out of sight, and restlessness filled him.

In sheer childish wrath, Robi took out his old toy cane and stood in front of the rails. Without any dialogue, he whipped them angrily and then stood with a fuming expression!

'Why don't you ever learn!' he exclaimed. 'Your disobedience and lack of interest in education are making me furious! I will punish you so much that you will never be able to talk! Well, you don't talk otherwise too, but this will make you speechless forever...'

He wished to hear a giggle, but nothing emanated from the emptiness.

Passing months till April 1881.
Tagore Mansion. Jorashako, Bengal.

Back in his own country, Robi was a man without the seal of a desired educational acumen. Yet, the impact of Western culture was too strong, and he continued to churn out his literary creations through various masterpieces. Thus lonely, dejected and obsessed with morbid fancies, he sought release in self-expression and felt obliged to please nobody!

That evening, as Bonomali, a subservient of Brajeswar, the head-servant, came into his room to keep a jar of fresh water, Robi stood near the open window and sneered, 'At last, what I write is my own! At last, what I shall create would be my own.'

The perplexed Bonomali stood with a blank face, while Robi noticed him. He came near him and whispered, 'Freedom first breaks the law and then makes laws which bring it under self-rule! Correct?'

Bonomali became even more scared, nodded his head in sheer confusion and ran away. Robi felt amused and closed the door. He took out a fresh notebook, opened the first page and wrote down a title for what was brewing within him…

Sandhya Sangeet… My Evening Songs.

The name, *Evening Songs*, indicated the wistfulness of the mood, as also the subconscious intimation that it was the sunset of his first phase of life. It was the sunset of the Rebellious Sun, to be reborn into a new dawn!

As Jyotirindranath and Kadambari left, the open-terraced roof and the adjoining room on the third floor became abandoned. In the absence of his Bouthakrun and Jyotidada, the emptiness of the place started to haunt him. In that painful separation, Robi, the rebel, occupied the room and the roof and made it his own. A few days later, even Satyendranath and Jnanadanandini left with the two children. Satyendranath had received his new posting, and he needed to join as a District Judge in a faraway province of India.

In his heart, a sermon echoed that he orated to Akshay Babu, the sole listener to his *Evening Songs* before they became publicly acclaimed. In the evening, after his takeover of the room, he told Akshay Babu, 'This is the room and this is the terrace where my journey of maturity has blossomed. I cannot leave it behind if I must indulge in my soulful endeavours. To be the one I want to be, I need this space to be my silent companion who would never interrupt me or dampen me. This space is my world of creativity.'

Robi's eternal liberation through the ecstasy in his poems, compiled within *Sandhya Sangeet*, was like the dance of a supernova as it dies with the brilliance of an unending beauty. Thus began a sonata which reverberated with the musical and lyrical conversation between Robi and his inner soul, the Rebellious Sun...

Robi asked, 'What are you writing in those concluding lines?'

The Rebellious Sun replied, 'These lines are my rebellion before I can perish happily, so that you can bloom. I must take her away, The Spirit of Evening, whom none can understand, yet she remains a mysterious beauty...'

'Read them to me,' commanded Robi.

The Rebellious Sun smiled and orated, 'Long ago, when I was a child, you wrapped me around with your affection as the evening envelopes the earth with its peace. Had the evening taught you its magic spell? For you looked into my heart and all the stars came out. You revealed my own hidden wealth to me, and without singing yourself, you taught me all the songs I know.'

Robi laughed as he listened, 'But this is just what is within you, my dear. I think there is much more hidden in that body of flesh and blood. Tell me more, my friend. I want to know what is haunting you!'

The Rebellious Sun replied, 'How can I say the unspoken lines? My dilemma is colossal. She owns me, but my heart has been touched by so many pure angels whom I couldn't gather the courage to speak up to. Yet, when I came back...yes, I came back to her. Then, she left me! She is gone—what more to say? They are gone—what song is left to sing? Only the heart wails its monotonous chant: they are gone, they are gone, leaving behind a wrecked heart. They are gone, and with them are gone the flowers and the birds and the light that brightens the day. Like a torn garment I am cast away...'

Robi again smiled and replied, 'Your poems are beautiful. You must metamorphose. The time is right to cross over to the new land of maturity. You are not the little boy anymore. You are a man now. You are a man who knows the sensitivities of youth!'

The Rebellious Sun answered, 'This is no single song or poem. These are my sentiments that come out through my emotional verses!'

Robi answered, 'Then continue to sing, my friend. This is you, the real you. Be fearless in your expressions. Your poems and songs would define you till eternity.'

The Rebellious Sun responded, 'Yes, I will write. My poems, "Suicide of a Star", "Hopelessness of Hope", "The Wails of

Happiness", "Invitations of Sorrow", "Unbearable Love"...all point towards love with sorrow, revelled in a bitter-sweet despair! Do you really think they would define me?'

'*Yes, my dear friend!*' answered Robi. '*They would define you! You are entering into a new world of maturity, and I am glad that this pain is defining you! Maybe, after ages and centuries, the human race would uphold these lines as the best definition of love!*'

The Rebellious Sun felt content. He answered to the only friend he knew, 'Yes, my friend. These poems I shall write. They shall become my definition.'

The murmur of unspoken ridicule continued to haunt him, but galloped on upon his unicorn of devastated heart across the lands of the three worlds: the world of his Bouthakrun, the world of Anna and the world of Lucy.

Unknowingly, within Robi germinated finesse and his works were the first few masterpieces. With a strange confidence, he presented those to the world, and the public reception was extraordinary. The murmur of ridicule slowly metamorphosed to a murmur of appreciation for a new star that had risen. The published works and the unpublished masterpieces created a sensation for the young bard.

Sitting alone on the open terrace roof, he laughed at himself and whispered silently, '*My life is in utter disorderliness. While left in communion with myself alone, I do not know how I slipped out of the poetical groove into which I had fallen. Perhaps, being cut off from those whom I sought to please, and whose taste in poetry moulded the form I tried to put my thoughts into, I naturally gained freedom from the style they had imposed on me... I had been searching in impossible places for that thing which was actually inside me!'*

Soon, Robi got invited to functions and social gatherings, and he felt happy with the sprouting of fame in his life. Even though he was yet to achieve something significant, the small bundles of reverence were like bursts of happiness.

During one such social gathering, at an invitation to a wedding, Robi met the acclaimed novelist Bankim Chandra Chattopadhyay. The crowd was ecstatic that evening, and everyone was enthusiastic to meet the great literary figure who was the chief guest for that evening. Robi sat among the guests and witnessed everything.

However, something unexpected happened. Just as Bankim Chandra was presented with a garland and was welcomed by the eminent hosts, he came up to Robi, took off the garland from his own neck and put it on young Robi.

Everyone became speechless, and Robi was startled. Bankim Chandra looked at his host and said with a smile, 'I present the garland to him. Ramesh, have you not read the *Sandhya Sangeet*?'

Despite the brewing acclaim and his liberation through his poems, Robi became lonelier with every passing day. The metamorphosis that youth brought in him was another concoction of strange emotional turmoil that was a shadow of social taboo. Thus, dejected and oppressed with his own self, Robi wrote to his father, who was, as usual, in the Himalayas...

Baba,

I have failed you on many occasions. I had travelled far and wide, yet I have achieved nothing. You had sent me to be a respected gentleman, but I have returned without any success. My heart grieves and repents. My tears don't stop because I could not bring that respect into your heart. For almost two years, I failed to attain stability. I know not what destiny holds in store for me, but I wish that this life of mine would not be useless.

Baba, with a flame of courage in my heart, I am writing to you. I seek your permission to go back to England to resume my studies. I would strive to be what you wish to see in your son. I pray that I would be worthy of it, in your eyes.

Yours truly,
Robi

The reply arrived in April 1881. It permitted him to travel back to England. In that undisclosed written conversation between a father and his son, Robi could see the face of his Baba saying…

Robi, my child, in life and in youth, we all commit some sins. However, they are not sins enough to demarcate us as sinful. Your failures are but momentary. My son, I am proud of who you are. Today, I give you permission to return to England and fulfil your wish.

On the evening before he sailed, Robi delivered his first public lecture in Calcutta. The topic was 'Music and Feelings', in which he illustrated his thesis with many songs. Being his first-ever public speech, he tried to demonstrate his finesse with his vocal illustrations.

His words echoed around the hearts and souls of the enthralled audience...

The function of music is to express what words fail to express...

April 1881. Reaching Madras.

Accompanied by a nephew, he started the journey on 20 April 1881. As soon as the boat left Calcutta, a sudden wincing emanated from the nephew. The boat sailed over the sea, but his heart sailed back home, to his newlywed bride.

'I cannot bear the pangs of this separation,' he whimpered. 'I don't know how long I would be away from her. The beautiful life that has just begun is getting trampled by this great expectation of mine! I wanted to go to England and do something meaningful. She supported me, even though her inner soul felt devastated. I know it. Yet, as I leave behind my everything, I feel the fruitlessness of such aspirations. Of what use would success be if I am not with the one I love so dearly? I have already started to feel sick for her, more than how sick I feel of the sea...'

The journey now began to get on Robi's nerves. He had himself convinced his own self to leave everything behind, once again, and go to England to fulfil a shattered dream. But the sobs of the nephew made him feel sicker.

By the time the ship reached Madras, the nephew had made up his mind. He didn't want to travel to England. However, he was scared. He approached Robi once again and said, 'Uncle, I am in deep fear. This faint-hearted retreat from our journey would bring so much criticism. But I just cannot go. I just cannot leave her behind...'

In that moment of great jeopardy, as they sat in the port of Madras, sweating under the heat of the glaring sun, Robi contemplated for an hour. Then, he got up, looked into the eyes of his nephew and said, 'I don't know why I am doing this, and please do not ask me for my reasons. But, yes, I have made up my mind too. Let us abandon this wretched journey. Let us go back. We would face whatever consequences would come. However, we would never regret this moment, ever.'

The elated nephew was in tears. He hugged Robi like a child and sobbed, 'Today, I realize that you understand the meaning of love like none other.'

Year 1881 onwards.
Returning to Jorashako. Off to Mussoorie. Thence, to the world of love.

At Jorashako, the return of Robi from Madras was like a tremor of an earthquake. The entire Tagore Mansion started to reverberate in a murmur of rage and contempt.

Within the quarters of the servants, the silent rumours began to echo: 'The young master has chickened out again! His elder brothers are furious, and their extended family is mocking his cowardly behaviour.'

Within the Inner Chambers of the women, the murmur had a different voice and a different pitch: 'He is so unlike his brothers or the other men of this stalwart family! The youngest pampered boy is proving to be a shame!'

None of those arrows could touch his soul. Nonetheless, Robi was concerned about what his Baba thought. Thus, he chose to embark upon a long and tiresome journey to where he was. The Maharshi was in Mussoorie. He was residing amid the lofty Himalayas at that point in time.

A petrified Robi reached his abode. With a thousand worries clouding his mind, he arrived in front of his Baba. The serene statuette of the stalwart man was like a marble figurine of God, and Robi stood in front of him like a helpless and worthless shadow of a colossal personality. Like a vagabond soul, he stood there without any success or pride that he could offer to his father.

'Come inside, my son,' said Debendranath serenely. 'Close the door, my boy. We need to talk. I don't want to see the anxiety on your countenance. Tonight, we must talk and none should know about it.'

The open sky was clear. Innumerable stars twinkled across the enormous vista above. Robi entered his father's room and closed the door. No one knew what happened behind that closed door.

Robi trembled in anxiety as he spoke, 'Baba, I have failed you on so many instances. When I tried to go back to England, I again failed you. I am a failure! Your youngest child is of no good...'

Debendranath looked at his son. Robi was trembling in fear, but his Baba showed no irritation. He touched his son's shoulders, perhaps like a father in a rare instance. He seemed pleased, and Robi was even more confused.

'Robi, this return of yours is like a divine providence,' said Debendranath. 'I don't want anything from you, my child. I never wanted anything lofty. I wanted you to be a happy child. Today, I see your happiness in something that the world doesn't understand. Yet it makes you happy. Follow your heart, my child. I know, one day you would make me proud in a manner that none in the lofty Tagore family could ever do!'

Robi held his father's hands and kissed them in an emotional upheaval. His tears didn't refrain from coming out, but he smiled and replied, 'Bless me, Baba! Bless me...'

'Go back home, my son,' said Debendranath. 'Seek your world and bring in the new sunshine.'

A smile flushed upon the face of the young man. The moonlight flooded the room and illuminated his face with a subtle and pure radiance.

At Villa 'Moran's Garden', Chandannagar.

After returning home, Robi felt a strange desire to be in the coveted company of his beloved Bouthakrun and his brother Jyotirindranath. With a free heart, he travelled to Chandannagar to be with them.

His arrival at the Moran's Garden Villa was like a gust of freshness in the life of Kadambari. As Robi entered the house, he was warmly greeted by Jyotirindranath. The first sight of the villa created a flush of poetic happiness in Robi. It was a big, rambling house that boasted of sprawling terraces and large windows. The house had an array of stone steps that led down to the banks of the Ganges.

As he entered his room, Monobihari, the manservant, brought in a glass of freshly made coconut water. Robi drank it at one go and said to him, 'It feels so great to be here again! And you are a lovely man.'

Monobihari returned a perplexed look at his young master. Robi gave him a flower that he had collected while he was entering the house, and said, 'This is for you, my friend.'

Monobihari was shocked and happy, but he didn't have words to say in reply. He grinned widely and then quickly went away.

That evening, Jyotirindranath sat with his brother while they spoke about various topics. Then he added, 'Robi, it feels so nice that you have joined us here. Soak in as much positivity from this journey and it will make you happier.'

Unnoticed by any, Robi's eyes involuntarily turned towards Kadambari, who was busy arranging the table for dinner. As their eyes met, she smiled. And in her smile, there was a touch of bliss. After many days, she felt content.

Before going to bed, Robi met her on the terrace and gave her back her notebook. He said with a smile, 'Bouthakrun...even I had taken care of this precious jewel. Indeed, their pages are like priceless treasures. I don't think they must ever be destroyed.'

That night, as he went to bed, an idea germinated within his mind. He took out his notebook and wrote down the thought. Then he pondered a while and wrote down the title... *Bou-Thakuranir Hat* (The Young Queen's Market).

From the next day onwards, Robi plunged into a mode of sheer elation. The first thing he did was to take a hearty swim in the Ganges. As the new morning unfolded, he told Kadambari, 'Bouthakrun, I am going for a swim. The water of the Ganges and the beautiful Ghat are summoning me to join them in their joy.'

Swimming in the river, while Kadambari watched him from the shore, he felt an ecstasy within his heart. The beautiful attachment had romanticism, even though untold to any, and brought the two hearts closer.

A few days later, as the rains played truant, Jyotirindranath said, 'Let us go on a ride over the river. The water seems so alive and vibrant. In this weather, the whole river seems so alive! Let us enjoy that beauty.'

When they boarded the budge row, Jyotirindranath took his favourite violin with him.

As the trio sat in their budge row, Robi sang his heart out while Jyotirindranath accompanied him with his violin. At the fountain of adulthood, he could now feel the intensity of a strange desire. On the other hand, Kadambari and Jyotirindranath, too, were inside a strange emotional upheaval. None of the three could escape the demons within.

After the idyllic holiday at Moran's Garden, Jyotirindranath, Robi and Kadambari returned to Calcutta. However, they didn't go back to the Tagore Mansion at Jorashako. They went and took residence at their house in Sudder Street. The act was like a mutiny, but the trio didn't care about what the entire world thought. Jyotirindranath was an open-minded man who had his own demons in life to deal with. Yet, they created a strange emotional turmoil.

House at Sudder Street.

The modest house was sufficient for the three of them. However, gossip began to murmur in the Tagore family, and the reverberations of those whispers started to reach the ears of Debendranath.

The stay at the house in Sudder Street had a bizarre spiritual effect on young Robi. He was a free man whose creative ideas were limitless. Deep inside his subconscious mind, the three ladies in his life played ruckus. Now, the fourth lady, his deceased mother, sought an entry into the already crowded heart of the poet. He had left behind Anna and Lucy. He was in the company of Kadambari, who owned him, but there was a stupendous social taboo that blocked everything. Yet, his mother, who was gone, whom he missed and whose company he craved, created uproar in his heart.

Even though in his most coveted company, Robi felt a weird despondency. He felt lonely. He felt sad. He felt alone. He felt...deprived of love. His sight got blurred. He felt a blanket cover his vision, even though he tried to create poetry to break away from the chains that pulled him down.

Then, one morning, as he stood by the balcony and watched the sunrise from behind the fringe of trees at the end of the lane, suddenly a covering seemed to fall away from his eyes. In that beautiful dawn, he felt as if the world was bathed in a wonderful radiance, with waves of beauty and joy swelling on every side. All his despair and despondency that had gloomed him and had weighed him down and had oppressed his spirit fell from him like a garment cut from end to end. Nothing in the outside world seemed trivial anymore. The invisible screen of the commonplace was removed from all things and all men, and their ultimate significance got intensified in his mind.

It was a prolonged experience that transported him to a different plane of awareness where he heard and saw everything not only with his ears and his eyes but with his entire being. In that endless wonder, he heard, '*Robi, my friend, leave everything behind. The whole world is your canvas. Create your own portrait in it. Mankind awaits your arrival. You are the bard in love!*'

The experience lasted for four days. Yet, it was an experience that metamorphosed him into a mature individual. In that heightened level of spiritual elation, everything seemed more vivid, real and beautiful. It helped him mature into who he became for the rest of his life...

At the end of the fourth day, the experience of extraordinary elation passed away, and Robi told himself, 'Finally, I have been able to cross over my borderline age!'

On that very day, he took out his notebook and wrote a poem that marked him as a poet beyond excellence. He named it *Nirjharer Swapnabhanga* (The Fountain Awakens). As he wrote the verses, his mind again whispered to his subconscious soul, '*Robi, your heart had been like a cave full of ice atop the lofty Himalayas! Today, as the sunlight penetrated it, that wall of ice has finally melted, and the caged water has now become free! It is rushing down like a cascade, leaping over the rocks and creating divine music along its journey!*'

Robi smiled and sighed, '*I was a lover of Mother Nature from my childhood. Midway, I had lost my path in the wilderness of my heart and had lost sight of that enigma. Today, I can again feel it.*'

As he spent the days in that house, he wondered how

he could experience such creative liberty and ecstatic happiness about Nature from within the dingy streets of Calcutta. He contemplated, '*If I can experience this here, then amid the boundless bounty of nature, I might feel an overload of this beauty within me!*'

Thus, as Jyotirindranath and Kadambari embarked upon a journey to Darjeeling, Robi vehemently accompanied them. The trip to the mountains was again something that illuminated a completely different corner within him. As Robi stood by the window and looked at the breathtaking view of the Kanchenjunga peak, a subtle emptiness filled his heart.

A visibly perplexed Robi contemplated, '*Why have I suddenly lost my vision? Why has that beauty of freedom and the splendour of poetic ecstasy vanished suddenly?*'

'*How is it possible that the lofty Himalayan landscape failed to ignite that spark within me that the dingy and congested street of Calcutta could do?*' he wondered. '*Perhaps that beauty in the vision and the music in that melody is hidden within the echo of the rhythm that beats in the heart of the Universe.*'

Hence, time moved on, but Robi gradually got moulded into the sculpture of a mature poet. Despite so, his attachment to Kadambari became more and more intense. But the young bard had outgrown her shadow of overprotection, and it pained her from within. Robi was now more extroverted and was growing beyond the fence of her own private boundary, where only she owned him!

So, two more years elapsed. Yet, the watchful eyes of the extended Tagore family began to scorn the visibly augmented intimacy between Robi and his Bouthakrun.

Summer and Monsoon of 1883.
Karwar, the southwest sea-coast of India.

Along with Jyotirindranath and Kadambari, Robi arrived in the land of fragrant cardamom and sandalwood. Their elder brother, Satyendranath, was posted in Karwar as a District Judge. The trio arrived to stay with his family.

In the bungalow, once again, Robi met his two little bundles of joy, Indira and Suren. They had grown up a bit. Indira looked at her beloved uncle, sat beside him and said lovingly, 'Now you must tell us stories every evening, for the rest of the days you will stay with us.' She lowered her voice and added, 'Did you forget about writing those letters to me?'

Robi smiled and embraced her. Then he whispered back, 'It is not yet time, my dear. But I will keep my promise.'

Jnanadanandini was happy to meet the members of her family. Kadambari mingled with her and helped her with her chores. However, an unseen social divide did exist between the two women.

Jnanadanandini again welcomed Robi with an open heart. The young lad had a special place in her heart, too. 'In this province, which is very different from Bengal, I am sure you would get varied resources for your creative mind. In this saline and humid country, I know, you would be able to seep in a poetic liberty.'

The words of Jnanadanandini were not incorrect. During the saline summers and the wet monsoons, in the coastal bounty of Karwar, Robi did find his liberty. During the months he spent in that land, he wrote his first important drama in verse, *Prakitir Pratisodh* (Nature's Revenge).

On a quiet Sunday evening, as everyone sat in the living room and a drizzle continued outside, tea was served, and they engaged in a light-hearted conversation.

Satyendranath asked, 'So Robi, have you been writing anything ever since you came here?'

Kadambari wanted to barge in with her comment and criticism. She had heard the lines he had composed. She wanted to refine them. However, as her eyes looked at everyone's faces, she gulped down her own words and sat quietly.

Robi replied, 'It is my first drama in verse. It portrays the eternal duel that goes on between the spirit and life, between beauty and truth, between reason and love...'

None but only Robi observed the two drops of tears that came out from Kadambari's eyes as she quickly wiped them away.

The trio returned from Karwar and went on to take residence at a Villa on Lower Circular Road. Again in the vicinity of the slums and the dingy lanes of Calcutta, Robi tried to focus on his world of creativity. Soon, they shifted back to their residence at the Jorashako Tagore Mansion. However, something else was becoming more and more conspicuous.

Jyotirindranath was engrossed with the failure of his business, and to forget his woes, he began to spend more time at the theatres of Calcutta and in the company of their actresses. The loneliness of Kadambari peaked. Her husband was estranged.

In that vivid emptiness and in the midst of the turmoil of youth, her heart came even closer to the man with whom she had grown up...her Robi. The erotic desires and upheavals of youthful longings made Robi mad, and that emotional turmoil oozed out through his poems in *Chhobi O Gaan*. He was a free soul now. He could now express his love and his desires without any fear!

The strange concoction of emotional hurricanes that each of these relationships suffered raised hordes of questions like poisoned arrows. Despite being away in the Himalayas, the watchful Maharshi Debendranath received the wounds from those assaults.

His verdict arrived at the elders of the family... *There is no reason why Robi shouldn't attend to both poetry and the family estates. But before that, the wild horse must be properly broken and harnessed. Find him a suitable match. He needs to get married.*

The commands reached his brothers, and soon Jnanadanandini returned to the Tagore Mansion. The eyes of the women within the Tagore Mansion had started carrying a contempt for Kadambari, and it even touched Jnanadanandini. Thus, the ladies of the household dragged Kadambari in the quest for a bride.

Perhaps it broke her even more. Perhaps it hardened her ailing heart to stone. Perhaps it created a demon inside her that was destined to consume everything! None but the fateful young lady held that truth as a secret within her heart.

Then, with familial pressure at its peak, Robi got married to Mrinalini Devi, then ten years old, originally named Bhabatarini. Marriage to Mrinalini was an episode that forged the rules of the orthodox society in the life of Robi. Yet, her turmoil in witnessing the relationship of Robi and Kadambari was destined to create a strange struggle within the newlywed couple.

Sadhana—Invisible Struggle of Love

'Let my thoughts come to you when I am gone, like the afterglow of sunset at the margin of starry silence...'

Flashback—
October–November of 1883...

The period was trying, and the time was flying, as Robi immersed himself in the ocean of his creative experiments as well as the depths of a unique bond of love. In a society that was conservative, his untainted youthful romanticism was far beyond the acceptable limits of society.

Thus, when the verdict from the Maharshi, his Baba, arrived, he transformed into a statuette of stone. He meekly submitted himself to the choice. The docile and obedient son was completely under the spell of his father's persona. Thus, as Jyotirindranath, Kadambari, Jnanadanandini, and a few other ladies prepared to visit a few families belonging to the Pirali sub-caste in the small provincial town of Jessore, Robi remained silent like a breathing mass of ice. As they exited through the main entrance, for a few moments, Robi's eyes collided with those of his Bouthakrun. In an ocean of devastation within her sight, Robi threw an unspoken question... 'Why?'

As an unmoved Robi sat inside his solitary room, at the Tagore Mansion, they went and did their job. The bride was chosen after a brief *paka-dekha* in Jessore. She was the daughter of Benimadhav Raichaudhury, an employee of the Tagore Estate. Robi knew everything was happening as per the directives of his Baba, who, despite being far away in the Himalayas, was omnipresent in the family. Soon, the family members returned. The marriage had been fixed, and the bride, with her family, was to travel to the Tagore Mansion, where the marriage was supposed to take place.

For the childless Kadambari, the chaos was like a tornado. She was heartbroken and was at her wits' end. Her husband's absence and his overindulgence with the ladies of the theatre were like piercing arrows. On top of that, Robi was no longer her sole possession. In a breeze of rogue wind, fate stole away every drop of romantic obsession.

A week or perhaps a bit more before the wedding, Robi sat beside Kadambari while the latter rested herself by the bedstead. Inside the rooftop room of his Bouthakrun, that evening there was none other. The weak flames of the lantern flickered in the breeze, while the wind carried a chill that pierced through the skin.

Kadambari looked at his face for quite a while and then said, 'Her name is Bhabatarini...'

Robi interrupted her and replied, 'I don't want to know it now. I know, she is thirteen years younger than me. She is a child. Bouthakrun, why is it that the bonds that bloom in companionship from childhood must get trampled with the onset of youth? Why can't a wild horse remain wild? Why can't an innocent child remain a child?'

She replied, 'Robi, life is a journey of disasters. It can't remain stagnant. If it does, how will it destroy? And, if it doesn't destroy, how will the "new" arrive?'

He asked again, 'This destruction is too much, Bouthakrun. It erases everything that the heart holds as special. As children, we had no worries. As that little boy, I only knew that in my whole world, I had one friend... You! Now, as time strides away, I have become so distant.'

She responded with a forceful voice, 'It was important. Robi, open your eyes and see how you have blossomed. The destruction of that childhood passion has crafted you as the man you are today! I am happy that I shall own you no more! I am happy that you would evolve out of the yore. Now, I can safely seek myself in the heart of a child again...'

Robi felt perplexed and angered at the bouts of depression that were slowly killing his Bouthakrun. He said sternly, 'And who would that be?'

She replied with a smile, as the shadow danced upon her face, 'That child would be Urmila.'

That night was subtle, and it created a new tentacle of destiny that was destined to sting her one day. Urmila was the five-year-old daughter of Swarnakumari, Robi's sister. In the solitude of Kadambari, the little child became like a beacon that she held on to.

Some bonds were meant to be fragile. The shattered hearts of Robi and Kadambari were connected by such a delicate bond of tragedy. So, as the days moved on, even though their hearts came closer, the hearts of the family members slowly floated farther and farther away from them.

December 1883. Jorashako Tagore Mansion…

Inside the Tagore Mansion, it was again time for festivities. Within the sprawling house, the unromantic marriage to the ordinary-looking, illiterate girl commenced. It was the first time that, perhaps, the dashingly romantic and dynamic Robi saw his bride and felt shattered.

As the fragrant garlands got exchanged, a pair of juvenile and scared eyes met a pair of large, expressive eyes that were brimming with an inner turmoil. The juvenile heart didn't know what storm was brewing. Thus, little Bhabatarini looked at her new husband, even though she was too young to understand the meaning of romantic love. As she plunged into the depths of that unknown ocean in his sight, her lips opened slightly and, for a brief moment, she giggled…

The grand wedding was complete, while a sinking Kadambari stood at a corner and witnessed that colossal shipwreck. In the eyes of the women of the Tagore family, she had unintentionally amassed a bountiful of scorn.

The wedding night was strange, perhaps the strangest that the young man could expect. Inside the confines of the high walls and the closed door sat the little girl who was far from being termed as beautiful. Under the veil of her saree, her fingers quivered with nervousness. She was just a child, and she didn't know what to expect.

Robi entered the room and sat upon the bed softly. In the silence of the night, he could hear the heavy breathing of his companion within that room. The entire episode of the wedding was a tumultuous one for his mind and body. The bride whom he just wed and whom he had just seen had perhaps created uneasiness within him. Yet, as he saw the small girl, trembling under the heavy veil, he felt pity and sad.

Robi sat beside her and said in a low but soothing voice, 'Don't be scared. There is nobody else. Please be at ease.'

The bride lifted her head a bit from within the veil and replied, 'Hmmm.'

Robi tried to make the situation a bit easier and added, 'You can get rid of that huge veil. Feel at ease. You can go and change into something more comfortable, if you want. Then we can talk a bit, maybe. We hardly know each other.'

After a little more time, the bride felt relieved. She went away and changed from her gaudy wedding attire. Wearing a soft cotton saree, she came back and sat on the bed. Her manners were rustic, with ordinary looks, but she had an intelligent reflection in her eyes.

Looking at the little girl, Robi floated away in his own mind into the world that he cherished the most ...his own childhood days. However, he forced himself back to reality and started speaking with her.

'You are a big man belonging to a huge household,' she said in a tingling voice that had a touch of melancholy. 'My father told me that I am being married into a stalwart family. I was scared. I have never been away from my village. I don't have a clue about what to do here.'

A few hushed giggles echoed back in Robi's ears. He had heard those amid the guests at the wedding ceremony... *The girl is a village commoner. Even her name is so rustic...*

Robi smiled at her and replied, 'Everything will be fine with the passage of time. From tonight, we shall try to be friends.'

The girl looked at her new husband blankly while Robi continued, 'From this moment, I want to give you a new name. It will be a name that will be yours forever. The entire world would know you by it. Will you be happy about it?'

The bride nodded her head lightly. Robi pondered for a bit. Flashes of his own broken past danced in front of his eyes. Then a name silently rang within his eardrums... Nalini.

Robi looked at the little girl and said, 'I name you Mrinalini... From this moment, this will be your new name that will redefine you as an undisputed and respectable member of the Tagore family.'

After a few moments of silence, he looked at her again and asked, 'Do you like it?'

The bride smiled with a wide grin, shook her head with force, and replied, 'Yes, it is beautiful. I love it. But, can I tell you something?'

Robi was a bit sceptical, but he consented. She added with enthusiasm and a serious face, 'I can cook well. I will cook good delicacies for you...'

A brief pause was shattered by bouts of laughter as the two of them chuckled heartily. The most unromantic wedding night thus melted into an ironic association of two souls to be bonded for a long journey.

Was it a shattering experience? Was it a sad episode or a happy one? Was it a mockery of destiny or a deep-rooted plan of fate? None knew the perfect answer...

Inside the dark, solitary quarter of her own sprawling room, Kadambari sat like a ghost of her own past. Her husband, Jyotirindranath, had become more and more estranged. His failure in business was an added wound to his own woes. He went bankrupt in his attempt to run a *Swadeshi* steamer company, in competition with the 'Flotilla Company' of the British. Yet, his acumen and his business instincts failed him, and so did his venture. As he lost his money and his prestige, he didn't succumb to his sorrow and seek solace within the family or within his wife. He sought comfort in his theatrical instincts and in the hoor of that esplanade... Binodini.

That night was a dark one. The moon was hidden behind the dark clouds. She sat on her bed and looked out through the open window. Downstairs, the window of the new bride, Mrinalini, was partially open. In the light of the lanterns, she could see inside the room. The little girl was sitting on the bed idly when Robi entered the room. In his hands was a pile of books. He kept them upon the bed, took a deep breath and spoke enthusiastically. Soon, a smile came upon the face of his new bride, and even Robi smiled back contentedly. Their voices were inaudible from the distance, but Mrinalini was visibly excited and, in her childish ecstasy, she got up from the bed and skimmed through the books that her husband had got for her.

With a desperate strength, Kadambari moved her eyes away and turned them towards the dark sky. The chunks of coagulated clouds gyrated to the passing winds. As she stared at them, the strange motion of the clouds and the darkness created a hallucination in her mind, and she floated into it. In that haloed vision, she saw...

Jyotirindranath was sitting inside the huge auditorium of the opera. It was a cloudy winter night, and everybody had gone home or had returned to their respective chambers. With a crystal bottle of whisky and a glass, he reclined upon a cushioned couch. His eyes were weary, and he was sad. He was seething in pain to recover his true worth. Then, from within the dark curtain, arrived a femme fatale, dressed in a gaudy attire. She swirled around him like an angel from heaven and then sat down beside him. She embraced him lovingly, while the latter rested his head on her bosom. In a loving voice soaked in pain, he cried, 'Binodini'...

As the shrill sound of an owl's hoot reverberated within the trees, her vision broke. Kadambari was in an almost intoxicated state. She got up from her bed and swayed unstably while she walked towards the cupboard. An hour ago, she had tasted a pinch of the white powder that she had secretly procured with the help of a trusted aide. Under the influence of that deadly matter, she felt a shattering ecstasy. She opened a private chamber within her husband's section inside the cupboard and scuffled through the contents.

'I know he will not return home tonight. His theatre draws him like a magnet... I know, Robi, you have a new playmate whom you can cajole now! I know, I must find out my own corner in this graveyard...' she howled softly within her caged body.

Then, from within a pile of folded clothes, she dug out a letter. With trembling fingers, she opened it and read it. It was a letter for her husband, Jyotirindranath. It was a letter of romance and a brave expression of love. It was a letter from Binodini.

Her darkest fears had come alive in that gyrating moment. Suddenly, she felt weightless and her body lost control. She realized that her mind was shutting down as she came crashing to the floor. As she fell down, her hand toppled the lantern and the latter broke upon the table. Alas, as she went into unconsciousness, she saw the letter being burnt away in the open flames!

That night, a domestic help noticed the flames and rushed inside the room to save the unconscious Kadambari from being consumed in a scandalous fire. However, despite her life being spared, she was completely devastated within her body and soul.

'The girl is naïve. She needs to be groomed in proper etiquette. Her education must go on in parallel with her sociocultural development. Her rustic upbringing needs to be erased to make her a worthy representative of the Tagore family. She must be polished,' came the verdict from Maharshi Debendranath.

The message was conveyed to the elders of the family, and then, Dwijendranath and Satyendranath communed to find a proper solution to the verdict.

'She must get enrolled in a good convent school,' said Dwijendranath thoughtfully. 'I guess The Loreto House Convent School for girls is the appropriate choice.'

'I agree with you,' added Satyendranath. 'Baba has sent his clear instructions, and the two eldest daughters-in-law have been assigned her guardianship.'

Robi felt a pang in his heart again. Within the few days after his marriage, the little girl had become like his ward, and he had been taking care of her in a strange fatherly manner. Within her untamed childhood, he could perhaps see a reflection of his own boundless childhood. Yet, the new verdict was about to change everything.

'I will get her enrolled in the school,' he replied to his elder brothers.

'But how can a daughter-in-law of the Tagore family attend classes like the other girls?' commented Dwijendranath. 'Baba is not very keen about it. You must speak with the school's authorities to arrange special classes for her. The family would pay for her uniforms, books, stationery, tuition fees, extracurricular activities and everything else.'

'Jnanadanandini feels that she must stay with us in our house,' Satyendranath added. 'In her company, the new bride would get an opportunity to become more and more pruned.'

Robi could only nod in agreement. The decision had already been made. He was a silent witness to the proclamation. He quietly went back to his own room. That evening, he told Mrinalini about the decision.

'Would I be able to do everything properly?' she asked. There was fear in her voice as her world was changing so quickly.

'Yes,' assured Robi. Again, a sense of pity engrossed his mind. Deep within, he sighed... '*Once more, a wild and free soul is being trampled under the tall pillars of societal values. Once more, a spontaneous and innocent child would be mechanized to become a social animal.'*

'Would you forget me?' asked Mrinalini innocently. She didn't understand the meaning of romance. Yet, a subtle attachment connected her with her new husband. He was like her mentor, her guide and her angel.

Robi didn't answer. He didn't know what to say. There wasn't any attachment within them. It was a mismatched marriage where an unknown and unnamed bond had developed. He smiled and went away. Before leaving, he stopped a bit, turned slightly and replied, 'I won't.'

The days moved, and the date of departure arrived. Escorted by Jnanadanandini, Mrinalini headed out from the Tagore Villa. A few moments ago, she had bid farewell to her new husband. In that brief moment, Robi tried to soothe her with his words, 'To the rest of the world, you are Mrinalini. In my words, I would address you as *Chhoto Bou*. I guess, this will not let me forget you...'

As she walked out and boarded the coach, Mrinalini shyly peeped out to get a glimpse of her husband. To her, he seemed like a nice and caring man, crammed between family values and the members of the huge, undivided family itself.

Robi stood at a corner of the veranda and sighed in his own self, '*I don't know how I will ever be able to love you. The germination of love never happens knowingly. Yet, through my instincts, I can feel that in my entire life, I shall be able to talk about my mundane days and my daily struggles with one person who would perhaps listen to me quietly and would never protest. I think my heart has discovered that companion in you...*'

In Kadambari's life, the turmoil was growing more and more. For the childless woman, the chaos was like a tornado. Even her adopted daughter, Urmila, the child of her sister-in-law, Swarnakumari, failed to pull her out of the bouts of depression. The heartbroken Kadambari was at her wits' end. Her husband's absence and his overindulgence with the ladies of the theatre were like piercing arrows. On top of that, Robi was no longer her own possession. In his nuptial bond, he now belonged to another woman. This came as a lethal blow to her almost ailing heart. For the rest of the world, it was an invisible struggle of love that was highly misunderstood.

Then, one day, another fatal blow befell. Kadambari was sleeping in the afternoon within her own room when a heartbreaking wail broke the silence like an explosion from hell. She got up hurriedly and came out of the room. There was sudden chaos among the servants and the family members, especially the ladies. The confusion was killing, and Kadambari failed to fathom the reason, but she understood that something deadly had taken place.

Then, a maidservant came rushing at her and screamed in terror, 'Urmila! Oh my god... Urmila has fallen down the stairs and has been injured! She is bleeding profusely. She will die...'

Kadambari rushed down the stairs and saw the gory scene. Her body trembled with shock as she saw the little child. The local doctor had been summoned, and every person was trying hard to stop her bleeding. Kadambari stood like a stone statue with her glance fixed upon the child. Within, her voice echoed... '*I wish, Kadambari, the child would have been you. I wish you had been meted out this fate, this gift of death. That would have been a lucky enough present for you!'*

'Where were you? Kadambari, how could you fail to even take care of the little five-year-old? How could you be so irresponsible, just because she is not your own? It is not that easy to be a mother! Your pang of feigned depression has taken the life of an innocent child,' the voices of the female members cut into her skin like the wounds of a million sharp daggers!

The death of Urmila was the last blow to her spine. In front of the stalwart Tagore family, she, Kadambari, became a howling shadow of misfortune and pessimism.

19 April 1884. Tagore Mansion, Jorashako.

Kadambari committed suicide four months after Robi married Mrinalini. The events that led to the devastating episode were equally devastating…

On that fateful night, as she sat on her bed, dressed for an evening with her almost estranged husband, her heart began to sink. The hours progressed towards the night, and the ship of hope started to sink. In that moment of despair, she hallucinated about the conversation she had with her husband, who was becoming more of a stranger in her life.

'We shall go on the boat ride tonight, and you shall feel better,' Jyotirindranath had said.

Kadambari understood that he would not return that night. Her sinking heart sighed, '*Your Robi is long lost in a golden sunset, while the man who had married you is lost in the glamorous lights of the opera and the beauty of the hoor on the stage. You are a ghost. This world is not your abode. You must seek solace in the world where ghosts truly belong!'*

She took out her notebook and the few personal letters, which were her only prized possessions. For one last time, she read them passionately and then destroyed most of them. But her hands trembled when she tried to burn the notebook and a few precious letters. She tucked them under her bed and sat like a stone statue. In her eyes, there were no more tears. In her body, there were no more fears.

Then, a slight knock on the door raised her alarm, and she quietly opened it. Outside, hidden in the shadow, was a shadowy figure who handed over a little paper pouch to her and quickly went away. Kadambari closed the door and went back to her bed.

She dimmed the lantern and opened the pouch. She took a handful of the white powder and, for one last time, looked at the mirror. In a moaning sigh, she looked at her own image and laughed, 'Hecate… Goodnight! Hecate… Goodbye.'

Then she swallowed the entire handful of the powder and closed her eyes. Soon, the hallucination deepened, and the visions of seventeen years came floating in. The clock ticked on, but the sounds and the voices became muffled gradually. Then, there was complete silence.

She had procured opium secretly, and she consumed a lethal overdose.

The almost lifeless body of Kadambari was discovered by the maidservants. The affair was a scandalous one, and she was kept in a solitary room to be nursed.

Everyone knew that her suicide was fatal. During the days and the nights, a helpless Robi paced restlessly across the veranda and the terrace. Yet, he could not utter a protest. The elders of the stalwart Tagore family were too high to do so. Only his tears were his companions.

Two days later, she passed away…

To hush up the entire episode and avoid a scandal, the coroner's report, letters of Kadambari and many other documents were destroyed at the behest of Debendranath. Even the family's account book had an entry: *Expenses towards suppressing the news of the death to the press—Rs. 52.*

A shattered Robi was left spellbound. The suicide of Kadambari made Mrinalini bleed within her heart as she saw, from a distance, her husband getting decomposed and withered with grief. In his revolt against the entire world, many of his timeless creations remained witness to his colossal grief.

But the obedient friend in him secretly took the notebook from her room and then set it on fire. As his tears dropped relentlessly, his heart sighed, '*I wish I didn't have to keep this promise. Bouthakrun, now that you have left me, I have kept my promise...*'

In that moment of apocalypse, perhaps a young Robi metamorphosed into Rabindranath Tagore!

'*She, my Queen, has died, and my world has shut against the door of its inner apartment of beauty which gives on to the real taste of freedom*', he sighed alone as he stood across the terrace. '*From today, Robi, the Rebellious Sun has set eternally. The companion of my childhood has departed; she has parted from me in tears—she had left her love for me. Those seventeen years of playing together. Those seventeen years of sorrow and happiness, those seventeen years of rains and springtime are like treasures! None knew me the way she did...'*

Kadambari's death ended an epoch. Nonetheless, it germinated an era for the 'Bard in Love'.

Nothing is perpetual in life. Neither happiness nor sorrow can be perpetual. Thus, Rabindranath stepped into a new world where destiny had some strange plans for him. And it began with a subtle bond that began to blossom between Mrinalini and him.

Yet, before it happened, there was a tornado that swept into the life of Rabindranath. Unable to fathom a way to overcome his pains and the colossal losses, he began to lead a vagabond's life. Astray with delusion and finding no reason to reconcile with life, he began to question how the sudden darkness in his life was preventing his soul from reaching out to a little source of light. Around him seemed a complete darkness.

As Rabindranath strolled restlessly across the open terrace, he wondered... '*How is it possible? In the midst of this unbearable grief, flashes of joy seem to sparkle in my mind, now and again, in a way which quite surprises me! That which I had held I was made to let go—this was the sense of loss which distresses me—but when at the same moment I view it from the standpoint of a subtle freedom gained, a great peace surrounds me.*'

In his words, he expressed in his letter to Amiya Chakravarty... '*With her death, it felt as though the earth had moved away from under my feet and the light had gone out from the sky. My world felt empty, and my life dull. I never imagined I would ever get over the delusion of this void. But that tremendous pain set me free for the very first time. I realized gradually that life must be seen through the window of death to reach the truth.*'

Through the conflict, Rabindranath saw himself in a new light. The omnipresent love was gone forever, yet it gave him an opportunity to love Nature, love the world and love the ones who loved him.

The restless Rabindranath, born from the oyster named Robi, sought to seek solace in the entire world. However, the silent yet elusively strong Mrinalini invisibly became his strength. Her grooming became appropriate, and she metamorphosed into a fine young woman who could ably represent the Tagore family. Nonetheless, the naïve and rustic girl got erased somewhere. It was the naïve girl whom Robi might have wanted to be a part of his own existence; however, in the refined Mrinalini, he could be a man beyond the cloak of the bard. So, in silence, she carried out her duties while her husband sought solace in her unknowingly. It was a strange love. It was a strange romance. Perhaps, a sense of duty and responsibility played a greater role in him towards his spouse, but somewhere within it, a flame of love was ignited.

On 25 October 1886, Mrinalini Devi gave birth to her first child, a daughter named Madhurilata and nicknamed Bela. In 1888, she gave birth to a son, Rathindranath. Some of Rabindranath's impeccable creations began to blossom during those years. His book of verse, *Kari O Komal,* was published in 1886, while *Mayar Khela* was released in 1888, which proved his artistic brilliance in musical drama.

In totality, both Rabindranath as a human being and

Rabindranath as a bard was evolving at a surprising pace.

1889–90: Years of Metamorphosis.

In the year 1889, Rabindranath took his family to Sholapur. Satyendranath was posted there as a District Judge, and the family of four started to stay with them. Parents of two, Bela and Rathi, Rabindranath and Mrinalini were again in the company of his Mejodada and his Mejo-Bouthan. It was in Sholapur that he wrote a drama in blank verse, *Raja O Rani.* Again, the inner conflict of struggling to recuperate from the colossal loss and the life that stretched ahead created the masterpiece within him.

Alas, the ever-restless Rabindranath was still a slave to the ghost of Robi. He continued to be the restless and unhappy poet who sought respite in relentless travels. Thus, from Jorashako, he moved to Park Street. He went to Darjeeling and then arrived in Sholapur. Yet, the traversing didn't stop. Leaving behind Mrinalini and his children, he headed to Poona and then went back to Calcutta. However, that too was short-lived, and he shifted to Ghazipur, in the Western Provinces. Here, he took his family, hoping the sojourn to be long. However, it failed to keep him long. Thus, a few months later, he skimmed through Calcutta, Shelaidah, Santiniketan, and then he finally went back to Sholapur. Despite all the restlessness, the harvest of his poetic soul kept blooming within his small notebook, and they later blossomed into the *Manasi* collection of poems.

In Sholapur, Satyendranath and his friend Loken Palit were contemplating a visit to England. The instant was strange, but again, the ghost of Robi tried to break into the life of Rabindranath. Thus, he insisted, 'I will come with you...'

Despite everything, Mrinalini continued to remain a faithful wife, who was perhaps much ignored. Yet, she knew deep within her heart, '*When he needs a shoulder to weep, when he requires a face to talk to, I shall be there.*'

Then, on 22 August 1890, he boarded the steamer to depart for England. Only his inner soul knew why he was going. Perhaps the ghost of Robi had whispered to him, '*Come, let us embark upon the voyage once more. Maybe Lucy is still waiting for you...*'

The subtle urge was not false. Hence, despite his bouts of seasickness, he reached London and headed to the house of Dr Scott. It was an abode where his thirsty heart wanted solace. Alas, tragedy was meant to be his constant companion, and thus, the coveted reunion failed to materialize. Lucy was no longer there. The family had moved away.

Rabindranath, despite all the calamities and the tragedies in his life, never failed to keep his promises. Thus, his letters to his niece Indira continued to encapsulate what his heart experienced. In one such letter dated 5 October 1890, he wrote, '... *One who has never known the turbulence of life, in whom the petals of the mysterious flower within have not opened, such a one may seem happy, may seem a saint, his single-track mind may impress the multitude with its power—but he is ill-equipped for life's true adventure into the infinite.*'

Thus, the ever-turbulent Rabindranath returned to India in November 1890, and soon after, *Manasi* was published. In 1891, Mrinalini Devi gave birth to a daughter, Renuka, and three years later, she gave birth to another daughter, Mira. It was the same year that Rabindranath composed the famous drama, *Chitrangada.*

As per the pressing desires of the watchful Maharshi Debendranath, in 1890, Rabindranath began managing his vast ancestral estates in Shelaidah and Orissa. As Zamindar Babu, he crisscrossed the Padma River in command of the *Padma,* the luxurious family barge (also known as 'budgerow'). He collected mostly token rents and blessed villagers who, in turn, honoured him with banquets—occasionally of dried rice and sour milk. He met Gagan Harkara, through whom he became familiar with Baul Lalon Shah, whose folk songs greatly influenced him. He worked to popularize Lalon's songs. He felt it as an inner obligation.

To his niece, Indira, he wrote once from Shelaidah: '*My work as zamindar took me on long distances from one village to another, from Shelaidah to Patisar, by large and small rivers and across beels. In this way, I saw all aspects of village life and felt a great keenness to understand the daily routine and varied pageant of their lives... Slowly but surely, I began to understand the sorrow and the poverty of the villagers, and I grew restless to do something about it. I began to feel ashamed of spending my days simply as a landlord, concerned only with my own profit and loss. So, I began to think about what could be done. I did not think helping them from the outside would help. I began to try and open their minds towards self-reliance.*'

The bard did keep his promise that he had made to little Indira many years ago.

The period 1891–95, his 'Sadhana' period, named after one of his magazines, was his most productive; in these years, he wrote more than half the stories of the three-volume, eighty-four-story collection *Galpaguchchha.*

Its ironic and grave tales examined the voluptuous poverty of an idealized rural Bengal.

Time moved on, and Rabindranath steadily transformed into a global citizen. Times were changing, and so were emotions and sentiments. Age was ageing, and the soul was getting older day by day. Amid everything, the relationship between Rabindranath and Mrinalini remained a very earthly one. In 1896, Mrinalini gave birth to her youngest child, Shamindranath.

Even though the world failed to ignite the flames of romance within them that could burn away all the sorrows, the couple lived together, had five children and continued to respect the nuptial bondage.

'The mismatch perhaps defines a match that was sketched by destiny,' sighed Mrinalini as she saw her husband getting drowned in his literary endeavours.

She knew she was never his *heroine*. She knew she was his...*saviour*.

Raktakarabi—A Red Oleander

'I seem to have loved you in numberless forms, numberless times, in life after life, in age after age, forever…'

Marching with the waves of Life Eternal
We must go forward with Truth as our Polar Star
And no thought of death.
Inclement evil days will pour over our heads,
But we must struggle on
To keep our Tryst with Him
At whose feet we poured the riches of our hearts
From age to age.

She was his saviour, with whom Rabindranath could be a regular human being. Maybe he couldn't be Robi within her, or he couldn't be the bard. But in her unique fragrance, he could become a creature of this world. Mrinalini knew that, and she also knew that physical separation from her would strengthen the bond between them. They were perhaps not meant to be united in romance; they were meant to be charmed in a farewell. In their mundane conversations, maybe she could churn out a glimpse of a strange romance.

In his letters to her, she could speak with him, smell his fragrance and feel his touch... Spread amid his words, in his mundane yet lively letters, she weaved her world as his lone companion.

Letter to Mrinalini: On-board SS *Shyam*: 29 August 1890...

We shall be at a place called Aden today. But we shall not be able to land there for fear of catching infectious diseases. We shall change ships at Aden. This time I have been quite seasick. My nausea was such that I could not eat a thing for three days. I was also very dizzy and could not get out of bed. I don't know how I survived.

On Sunday night, I felt my spirit leave my body to come and see you. I saw you sleeping on one side of the large bed, next to you were Beli and Khoka. I caressed you and whispered in your ears, 'Chhoto Bou, please remember that on this Sunday night, I left my body to come and see you. I shall ask you on my return from England if you saw me too.' Then I kissed Beli and the baby and returned.

Did you think of me when I was ill on the ship? I was dying to return home to you. These days, I am convinced there is no place like home. I am not going anywhere after I get back from this trip.

...There are a couple of small girls on our ship whose mother is no more. They are going to England with their father. My heart goes out to them. Their father watched over them closely—they don't know how to look after themselves. They dash out into the rain,

and if their father asks them not to, they insist they like it in the rain. Their father smiles. I guess he feels sad to deprive them of their fun. They remind me of our children. I saw Beli in a dream last night. I saw that she is on the ship, looking splendid. What shall I bring them from England? If you answer this letter as soon as it reaches you, I might get it before I leave. Don't forget the post to England leaves on Tuesdays. Kiss the children for me, will you?

Letter to Mrinalini: On-board SS *Masilia*: 6 September 1890…

I wrote to you the day before yesterday. I am writing again today. You may get both these letters on the same day; what is the harm? We shall be landing tomorrow—all the more reason for writing to you today. I will be able to write again on reaching England. In case there is a slight delay in my writing to you over all this movement, please don't be upset. It is not difficult to write from the ship, but once we have landed, it is not always predictable where we shall be. There may be a day or two when I may not be able to write. We shall be in England tomorrow.

We can at times see Europe's coast at a distance. There is Greece on our left and an island on our right as our ship goes down the middle. The island seems very close to us—there are hills and houses and a large town somewhere—I can see the houses quite clearly through the binoculars. The town looks rather nice with its white houses in the middle of the blue hills. Do you not wish to see all this, Chhoto Bou? One day you must come too. Are you feeling happy to think of that day? What you see will be beyond your dreams.

...We shall arrive in Paris tomorrow. There is so much food served on the ship that I may have put on some weight. I hope to see you looking well and fat when I am back, Chhoto Bou. The car is now with you. I hope to go out in it every day. Don't just lend it to others. Last night there was a drama on board our ship—there are quite a few fun things happening. Tonight is our last night here.

After his return from England in 1890, Rabindranath began managing his vast ancestral estates in Shelaidah (today a region of Bangladesh). With his wife and children in Sholapur, he traversed across the Zamindari estate all alone.

Letter to Mrinalini: Shazadpur: Year 1891...

It has been one month since I came to stay here. I have found that I can barely manage a month away from home, and that too only if I have plenty to do. I long to return home after that.

There was a storm here last night. I could not sleep for a long time with the noise of the howling winds. You may have got this storm. It rained a lot yesterday. The waters have risen considerably. The mustard fields are all submerged. One foot more and the same would happen to our garden.

Please tell me if you are taking a walk on the roof twice daily. And tell me also if you can do the other things required for your health. But I rather suspect you are just comfortably stretched on an armchair with a novel. Have your headaches gone?

Letter to Mrinalini: Shelaidah: Year 1892...

I got your letter just as I was leaving Shelaidah this morning. It made me sad. But the thought of your returning to Calcutta cheered me up. Otherwise, I would not have come to Calcutta now. I am not feeling too well either and wish that you were with me. I am sure in my mind that it would be for the best that all of you stay in Sholapur for as long as possible. I had hoped that the children would study well there and grow up healthy. Anyway, not everything can be in one's control. We have to make do with what comes our way and dutifully do the best we can under those circumstances. That is all that is humanly possible.

Please do not nurse discontent within yourself, Chhoto Bou; that does more harm than good. Let us just carry on resolutely with contentment and a smile. With my brooding temperament, I know that I suffer unnecessarily. I want you to stay happy; otherwise, our prospect looks bleak. You know, my dear, how intense I am by nature. But you know how hard I work to keep calm. Please help me overcome my discontent, and please never join me in it.

If you are already on your way, I shall see you when I am in Calcutta this time. I shall try to arrange for you to come with me to Orissa. It is a very healthy place. I have already told Baba what I want to do, and I think he understands. I may get my way if I talk to him once or twice more—still, it is best not to raise our hopes. I have a feeling this letter may reach you while you are still in Sholapur. It may be eight or ten days more before you can start. Let's see.

My boat is slowly moving along the whole day. It is already evening, but we have not yet made it to Pabna. Once we are there, we shall have to go on for many more miles by palanquin.

Letter to Mrinalini: Year 1899...

You know from my letter to Bela that I was not able to come today. I have stayed home. The post arrived; there were three letters, but none from you. I did expect one, but wondered if by divine chance you could have written one by mistake! The joy of living separately is in writing letters to one another. It can be more rewarding than being together. When we write letters, we can come closer to each other with only a few words, and get as much of each other as possible by way of those few words.

What we say to each other when we meet can fade away in the instant excitement of meeting each other. Really and truly, writing letters can become a deeper and more intimate experience for knowing ourselves than just seeing each other. Don't you agree?

Letter to Mrinalini: Calcutta: December 1900...

I do constantly try not to worry about our children. It is our duty to see to it that they are well-behaved and that they get a good education. Beyond that, it is a mistake to dwell upon them. They will grow up to do their life's work in their own way, be it good, bad or indifferent. It is, of course, true that they are our children, but they are also individuals in their own right. We will not have much control over the way they live their lives. Let us do our duty to them, but let us not expect too much from them. It is in God's hands how they turn out as human beings. It is from a certain vanity that we expect the best from our own progeny. We have no right to do that. After all, are we all that about other children who have hard lives?

The future is uncertain, no matter how we live. Therefore, it is only sensible that we should simply do our duty and not think of the outcome. We have to forever learn to take both good and bad—and we must restrain ourselves every time there is an urge to deviate from that path. We have to understand that we do not belong only to this life of ours. We have our past, and we can have no prior knowledge about our future. Therefore, all that is possible is to do our work diligently, wherever we are and whatever the work is. We must also try to be happy and make others happy. If, after that, we fail, it should not matter to us. We must accept and remember that the results are in God's hands once we have done our part. We must at least try to free our minds from expectations.

Letter to Mrinalini: Calcutta: December 1900...

I am so delighted to get all of two letters from you today. Unfortunately, I am unable to respond...because I must go to Bolpur today. I have read out to my father my address for the Seventh Pous celebrations. He has asked me to expand it a bit here and there. I have to get down to that now. There is only an hour left to finish it.

Please don't work any harder for my happiness. Your love is enough. But it would be very nice if you and I could work together and think together with one mind. I know that it cannot always happen, even if we wish it. It will make me happy if you could join me in all that I do—and give me much joy if you agree to learn what I want to learn... It is easier to move forward if we are united. I don't wish to leave you out of anything I do, but I hesitate to thrust my will on you. It may not be possible for you to agree with my wishes and inclinations every time—I would not worry about it. It is good enough if you spare me sadness wherever possible, and sweeten my life the way you do with your love.

Year 1901. Santiniketan, 'The Abode of Peace', and onwards...

On 22 December 1901, Rabindranath inaugurated his school at Santiniketan with five pupils, including his eldest son, and as many teachers. Mrinalini supported her husband financially by selling off most of her jewellery to fund the project on their own. The bard had matured in many ways, both mentally and spiritually. To bring forth a vision that had germinated within his mind, he established an *ashram* with a marble-floored prayer hall—the *mandir*—an experimental school, amid groves of trees, gardens and a library.

Things suddenly started to move at a precarious pace in their lives. Rabindranath, the man who had slowly matured into a more composed soul, saw how quickly his entire world was changing. However, he was unaware of the whirlwind that was about to come very soon. On 15 June 1901, Mrinalini and Rabindranath married off Bela. Then, on 9 August, they married off Renuka to

Satyendranath Bhattacharya. Despite being the bard with a wayfaring soul, he couldn't escape the clutches of societal rules. Thus, the two daughters were hurriedly married even as they were mere children.

In their little house, where the fledgling family was slowly setting up their nest, on a damp and solitary evening, Rabindranath sat beside Mrinalini and wondered how life had been. Despite every struggle, she had undeniably been an invisible inspiration who shaped his maturity. He looked at her and smiled, 'Today, I feel happy. The bond we share is different. The love we garner is different as well. Yet, in you I can confide. Yes, in you, I have found a way out from the shell of Robi to become Rabindranath.'

The unspoken fact remained that during the last eighteen years of their marriage, after the death of his Bouthakrun, something extraordinary had happened...

His book of verse *Kari O Komal* (published in 1886), the novel *Rajarshi* (1887), the operatic play *Mayar Khela* (1888), the phenomenal play *Raja O Rani* (1889), *Manasi*, the collection of poems (1890), the plays *Bisarjan* (1890) and *Chitrangada* (1892), his collection of poems *Sonar Tori* (1894) and his major novel *Chokher Bali* (1903)...together created a global identity for the bard.

As Mrinalini had become his silent shadow, Rabindranath had unknowingly created his masterpieces!

Was it the result of an unrecognized and unstated 'love' that had germinated unknowingly? None knew it. None understood it.

Nonetheless, somewhere destiny smiled at the contrast it had created. Yes, Rabindranath's best creations were born when he was always nestled in the heart of his silent saviour, Mrinalini. She was a woman who had been self-effacing and gracious and had looked after him with unstinted devotion, and had borne him his children. Despite living in an aristocratic society, she dressed very simply and wore almost no jewellery. From her rustic background, she had refined herself into an educated woman who was proficient in Bengali as well as in English, just to remain in the eyes of her husband.

Alas, the years passed away too soon, and when a bond of 'love' was about to be ignited, something catastrophic happened…

By the middle of 1902, Mrinalini became seriously ill. Subsequently, Rabindranath took her and moved back to Calcutta from Santiniketan. Despite all efforts, doctors failed to identify her disease.

When the final moments were at the doorsteps, Rabindranath understood that the shipwreck was inevitable. He sat beside her, constantly nursing her during those days. He refused to engage a professional nurse to take care of her.

Day and night, he sat beside her bedside, his hand-fan gently moving above her. His face was distraught. His spirit asked him, *'Who will be your friend now?'*

One night, a frail Mrinalini looked at him and said, 'For almost two decades, I tried relentlessly to become your worthy companion. But, even today, as I feel myself sinking, I still see myself as that little rustic girl who sat beside you on her wedding night and said… I can cook well. I will cook good delicacies for you...'

She paused a bit to breathe and then added, 'Did I succeed in meeting all your needs? Did I cook well for you? Did I live like a true wife?'

Tears rolled down the face of Rabindranath. He kissed her forehead and replied, 'You have done everything beyond what was needed. I failed you many times. I failed to give you what you deserve truly. Alas, I am still greedy! Even tonight, I want to ask you... What will I do without you? Who will be my guide? Who will be my saviour? Who...'

Mrinalini held his palm and closed her eyes. A serene smile appeared upon her countenance.

Then, on 23 November, she passed away at the tender age of twenty-nine. Rabindranath had devoted himself to nursing her during the last two months of her life. A strange sentiment played ruckus with the couple, where the invisible love had perhaps metamorphosed into a sense of eternal duty.

He spent the entire night on the terrace walking up and down, having given strict orders that no one was to disturb him.

The ruthless onslaught was complete, and Rabindranath was again a vagabond Bedouin who stood in hallucination of an oasis to quench his thirst and kill his pains. A few days after Mrinalini's death, he found a bunch of letters amid her belongings. They were safely kept and preserved like treasures. Rabindranath held those letters in his own hand and wept profusely.

Sitting upon the floor, he wiped his tears and sighed, '*Oh, Almighty! I pray that her memory may bring order into my life just like she had brought order into this family.*'

A year after her death, Rabindranath published a volume of poems in her memory, titled *Smaran*.

'*The stride of ruthless "death" has walked into our lives,*' he moaned as he stood alone, once more, on the dark terrace. *'Who knows what else it will take away with it...'*

Then, destiny swept him away into a state of despair as he watched his beloved second daughter, Renuka, suffer from a prolonged illness and die at the tender age of thirteen in September 1903. Four months later, a favourite poet, who was like his own son, Satish Roy, passed away. In 1905, Maharshi Debendranath breathed his last, while in 1907 his youngest son, Samindra, died of cholera.

Thus, within the short span of a few years, Rabindranath saw the merciless onslaught of death upon his beloved people. He was left devastated.

In the hope of peace, Rabindranath continued to roam the world, in his literary rendezvous, to seek solace in the Almighty through his timeless poems. As his personal losses eroded his inner soul, his creation, his beloved Santiniketan, continued to bloom while he himself plunged into the depths of work to remain alive. He was most content as the reclusive poet and the teacher of little children who lovingly named him Gurudev.

November 1913: Nobel Prize in Literature...

Then, in November 1913, he learned he had won that year's Nobel Prize in Literature. The ecstasy was huge, but it remained cloaked within the shroud of his personal tragedies. The entire country went ecstatic. The little students at Santiniketan didn't know what the Nobel Prize meant. However, they were elated that their Gurudev had been recognized for his works by the entire world. Inside his heart, Rabindranath too felt happy and content. His patriotic persona was also delighted as he received the recognition for his country. Still, the quiet, shy and solitary bard felt something weird.

He even wrote to Rothenstein, *'The perfect whirlwind of public excitement it has given rise to is frightful. It is almost as bad as tying a tin can to a dog's tail, making it impossible for him to move without creating noise and attracting crowds all along. I am being smothered with telegrams and letters for the last few days, and the people who never had any friendly feelings towards me nor ever read a line of my works are loudest in their protestations of joy. I cannot tell how tired I am of all this shouting, the stupendous amount of its unreality being something appalling. Really, these people honour the honour in me and not myself.'*

Above everything, the awarding of the Nobel Prize to Rabindranath was received everywhere with a shock of surprise and converted him from an individual into a symbol—a symbol of the West's grudging recognition of Asia's submerged potential and its imminent resurgence.

When 'Love' Came, from Beyond...

Thenceforth, a decade and a half swept away while the bard in 'love' wept within his heart as he continued to churn out masterpieces. His life metamorphosed into a symphony of tragedies, but Rabindranath found solace in the spirituality that was born from his deeply experienced sorrow and loneliness. Rabindranath, despite being a forward-thinking man, always blamed himself that he had pushed his youngest daughter, Mira, into an unhappy marriage with Nagendranath Ganguli. Thus, once her separation happened, he never forced her to return to her husband. It was a retribution that he sought within himself for the mistake he had made.

Amid all the turmoil, in his struggles to manage the school and in his relentless battles to stay afloat financially, something magical happened. As age progressed and the bard crossed fifty-six years of his life, a new light shone in.

Amid the numerous postal correspondences, one letter reached Rabindranath and overwhelmed his mind...

Dear Robi Babu,

I have read all the stories of your book 'Galpaguchchha' and have followed each of them. The only one that I couldn't quite understand was 'Kshudita Pashan' (The Hungry Stones). Tell me, why didn't that old man, who had once mentioned the Iranian maid, finally tell her story? I would love to hear it. Please write about it sometime, will you?

Again, the story of 'Jai Parajai' ended with Shekhar marrying the princess. But my elder sisters insist that Shekhar had actually died. Please write that Shekhar did not die and was married to the princess. Okay? If Shekhar really died, then I will feel very sad indeed.

I want to see you ve..rr...yy much. You must visit us sometime. You must; otherwise, I won't talk to you ever again. And if you do come, then I'll let you sleep in our bedroom and give you our dolls.

Ranu

Rabindranath read the letter twice. There was a certain amusement hidden within the letter that lifted his spirit.

The letter was from a girl, probably a young girl from Varanasi, whose innocence was reflected in her words.

'*Robi Babu...*,' sighed Rabindranath. '*The sentiment in the expression makes me feel a pang in my heart. Who is this girl? She has not even mentioned her surname. Without the fences of a formal regard, the letter and her voice are superfluous...*'

Soon, another letter from this little girl made Rabindranath laugh. After a long time, he could laugh and that too with someone who addressed him as Robi. The bouts of thunder were growling outside. Rabindranath came out upon the veranda and looked beyond into the open fields. As the showers came down, he stretched his hands and bowed his head to welcome the freedom of the raindrops. A smile emerged on his lips that were safely secured within his white beard.

Some voice said to him from within, '*I shall reply to her. In her mysterious persona, she appeals to me with a mystic purity.*'

Amid his poetic, political and social escapades, Rabindranath became engrossed in multiple things. Moreover, the duties towards his school in Santiniketan remained paramount. It was his personal challenge to the world that his vision was truly mammoth.

Then, in the midst of preoccupation and uncertainty, another letter arrived from Varanasi...

Dear Robi Babu,

I have been very angry because you hadn't written to me for so long. Now I am really glad to have received your letter. Do you know what my actual name is? It's Priti—rather a lovely name, isn't it? Everybody calls me Priti at school. But you can call me Ranu, just Ranu.

It's because I myself am very fond of it. I have many other names as well—would you like to hear them? They are Rani, Raja, Baba—all of them are nice, aren't they? The lecture that you had given on 'The Doer Wills the Dead' was published in the magazines Probashi *and* Bharati. *My mother, Babuja, Babu and Asha, all those who read it, thought it was a good piece of writing. I too tried to read it but couldn't understand a single word. Possibly because it was a difficult piece. Do you know, I fell ill a few days ago? But I am much better now. You must visit our house sometime. We'll never leave this house because this is our own. It's not a rented house. But you must inform us before you come here. Then I'll take leave from school and go to the station to fetch you. Please send me a reply soon, and make sure that you don't misplace this letter. See, I have written this letter on such beautiful paper with flowers on it.*

I am writing my home address once more.

235 Augustya Kund
Banaras City

P.S. Why don't you write stories anymore?

The address in the letter made Rabindranath ponder. He remembered that the address was that of a Sanskrit Professor Phanibhushan Adhikary. He remembered that Phanibhushan had several children, but he couldn't recollect who Ranu was. He could only recollect that the eldest girl-child was named Asha.

A while later, the third letter arrived, and it made the ageing bard chuckle like a child. In the lines and overtones of the letter, he was perhaps rewinding into a child again...

Dear Robi Babu,

Please don't be angry with me for not writing to you for so long. Actually, I had been ill. But I am quite alright now. Please, don't be angry with me. Our Puja Holidays have started today. The school will reopen on 31 October. Tell me, do you really have any other work apart from writing letters? I don't see you writing any more stories either. Nor do you go to school. Actually, I seem to have much more work than you. I take lessons from my teacher till nine o'clock in the morning. I attend school till four in the afternoon. Then I return home and take Hindi lessons from Panditji. And in the evening, I do my homework. Listen, I will not call you ugly when I see you. After all, the pictures show you as rather handsome. But you must be even better looking than those photos! I have quite a handsome friend, don't I? You might not have a good-looking friend, though. I think I'll feel very happy to see you. But you must come and live with us sometime. No, you can't stay anywhere else. Tell me, did you live in a boat on the Padma River or in a house on its bank? I wish I could be there. I really do...!

Amused by the constant insistence, Rabindranath had replied, '*You may get scared on seeing me, I look quite frightful with my beard and moustache, and I am very old. Almost fifty-seven years.*'

The reply from Ranu was again like a gust of freshness: '*Surely you can't be that old. Do poets ever grow old? You are only twenty-seven. At least that is how I think of you. You will never grow older than that.*'

Lost in her innocence, maybe the bard again fell in

'love' with himself. Maybe he started to re-live his own childhood, whose reflections were visible in the words of Ranu and her letters.

The death of Bela in 1918 was like a final blow to his wounded heart and mind. Despite being married into a significant family, Rabindranath knew that Bela's marriage had been a mistake. Her husband lived a rogue life, and an ailing Bela distanced herself from the entire world.

On the day she died, Rabindranath visited her house, but couldn't gather the courage to enter and see her corpse. He placed the flowers near the doorsteps and quietly moved away. Tears had dried within his eyes, and he was unable to cry.

He reached Jorashako and then headed straight towards Bhawanipur. As he reached 35 Lansdowne Road, he rushed in with the cry, 'Where is Ranu? I have come to meet her...'

It was the house where Phanibhushan and his family were staying for an interim period. The ailing man had come for medical treatment. The residents of the family recognized the bard, and soon a small crowd gathered around him.

Then, the little eleven-year-old, with a rosy complexion, innocent doe-like eyes and very curly hair, came in... And she was completely nude!

Yet, in the eyes of the bard, she was like a hoor from heaven. She was like the angel, pure to the core, who had the elusive power to erase his colossal loss, the death of Bela.

The girl clasped his hands as the bard stood speechless. Then he said, 'So you are Ranu, aren't you?'

'And you are Robi Babu, and you have kept your word after all. You have finally come to our house!'

Soon, the girl's mother came in. She was visibly shocked and immediately sent Ranu inside to get dressed. As his trance broke, Rabindranath felt somewhat embarrassed. The last nine months of communication over numerous letters gave birth to the angelic meeting. And like every birth, the child was bare. Yet, there was a pureness that shadowed all that was vulgar.

Rabindranath gathered his composure and invited the family, 'Adhikary Babu, if you wish to regain your health, why not come and stay with your family at Santiniketan! The air, water and climate are all pure. I insist that you come.'

Thus, the much-coveted visit commenced, and Ranu stayed in the shadow of her beloved Robi Babu. In the lap of Mother Nature, she moved around like a free bird in the wild. She even discovered a playmate in a lone deer that roamed around in the mango grove and along the banks of the Khoai River. From a distance, Rabindranath watched her and felt a deep fulfilment. She was like his cherub who was destined to liberate his ailing heart.

Then, after the dreamy days slowly moved on, the passage of time pulled in the moment of parting. It was time for Ranu and her family to leave for Varanasi. She was heartbroken and sobbed profusely. Santiniketan had become her true abode, and her Robi Babu had become her mismatched soulmate. Yet, she had to leave, somewhat forcibly. But, things were to change very soon.

Ranu Adhikary came to Santiniketan from Varanasi many times. In fact, she had run away from home as a rebel against her father's constant forbiddance. Once, Rabindranath was planning to go to Dehradun with his full family for a summer vacation. The sudden arrival of the little girl was alarming. However, Rabindranath understood her inner turmoil and wrote to her father, asking him not to worry. He inducted Ranu into the fraternity and even took her on the vacation along with his family.

The arrival of Ranu Adhikary at a tender age was again a disruptive episode. She began to grow up in that serene atmosphere and stole the heart of a man who had lost so much. A subtle relationship developed between them.

Later, in his famous drama, *Raktakarabi* or Red Oleander, in the year 1926, Rabindranath conceived a love triangle with himself and her as the protagonists. The beauty of her association with Rabindranath remained in the blossoming of a subtle relationship that bloomed like a Red Oleander in the bountiful garden of Santiniketan.

It was love and friendship that were pure and ethereal. In his human persona, she was the reflection of his lost children, especially his daughter. In his creative world, she reflected the image of the one lady who had been his inspiration. She represented his beloved Bouthakrun. In her eyes, he was her 'hero'. In her heart, he was her soulmate who was beyond the boundaries of age and mortality.

Ranu didn't want to call him Robi Babu. It was a name that quite a few others also used to address him. Thus, she wanted something that would be hers exclusively. As she sat with Rabindranath, he said, 'Many years ago, I was Bhanusingha, the Rebellious Sun. With time, that sun had withered. However, you can call me Bhanu Dada. In you and your worlds, maybe that Rebellious Sun will get reborn.'

So, Bhanu Dada became the name that solely belonged to her. Ranu metamorphosed into the soul whose presence made the bard alive once again. It became a unanimous fact that reverberated across the entire Santiniketan.

In a letter to Ranu, Rabindranath wrote, 'Suddenly you came into my life as her (Kadambari Devi's) emissary; my deep affection for you is at her behest. This is my reward. My enthusiasm for work doubles at this, my fatigue disappears, and the sky of my mind lights up.'

The uncanny similarity of her appearance to Kadambari Devi was even felt within the Jorashako household when she visited the place with Rabindranath, and a maidservant screamed with fright on thinking her as the ghost of Kadambari.

Rabindranath experienced a wonderful touch of 'love' in Ranu. However, he wanted her to have a good and stable life. Thus, he confided in her mother and even took away many of his letters to her to avoid any misunderstanding. Several of his later works were truly inspired by her. Yet, he felt happy that he could see Ranu mature into a woman of substance.

In his verses of *Sandhya O Prabhat* (Dusk and Dawn), Rabindranath celebrated the subtle union of the two in the last few lines. The lines perhaps defined the sensitive bond he shared with Ranu...

Let the shadows of one
Caress and kiss the light of the other,
Let the 'Puravi' of one bless the other's 'Bibhash'
Before moving on.

Ranu Adhikary got married to industrialist Sir Biren Mukherjee, and she became Lady Ranu Mukherjee.

She lived a celebrity life in her later years and became a patron of the arts. In the year 1933, she helped found the 'Academy of Fine Arts' in Calcutta.

Sonar Tori
The Golden Boat

Yatri—The Vagabond's Escapade

'When I go from hence, let this be my parting word, that what I have seen is unsurpassable...'

Years 1921–23; Sriniketan: The dream of an 'Abode of Well-being'...

Rabindranath had made a choice in his life. There was an ocean of sorrow and difficulties in his life. To remain afloat, he created his own Golden Boat that, in Bengali, sounded like 'Sonar Tori'.

In that Golden Boat, he sailed on by submerging himself into work and into the joy of creating literature. He had been a part of the Freedom Movement. He had established Santiniketan. He travelled across to Europe and America and lectured on his beliefs. Through his travels in the early periods of 1920–21, he endeavoured to raise funds and enlist support for his dream institution. Many scholars who shared a similar interest in the study of cultures and shared his views on the unity of the human race became closely acquainted with him. Professor Sylvian Levi of Sorbonne University even accepted his invitation to become a visiting professor at Visva Bharati in the autumn of 1921. The efforts were yielding fruit, and his struggles were reaping the crops of success, slowly and steadily.

Rabindranath became a busy man, maybe to evaporate the tears of blood. In that Golden Boat, the lone suffering soul rebelled to kill his loneliness. Only through his various endeavours could he win that battle, both inside and outside.

He was a warrior poet whom destiny failed to cripple.

Another such brilliant dream was his dream of Sriniketan (or 'Abode of Wellbeing'). He deep dived into converting that solo dream into a global vision. Commencing a scientific agricultural process within a model village and a conclusive rural reconstruction plan were the other pillars of the idea. The Rebellious Sun was once again blazing on to redefine history.

It is not enough to try to remove wants; you can never remove them completely from the outside; the far greater thing is to rouse the will of the people to remove their own wants... He fearlessly expressed his views to make the downtrodden masses of his motherland more independent and self-reliant.

Of course, turning out songs is my proper work. But those who are unfortunate and cannot afford to limit their choice to the work they can do must also bear the burdens of the tasks they cannot do... He expressed this in the year 1921.

Fortunately, with good luck in the period of 1920–21, during his visit to America he met Leonard Knight Elmhirst, who was graduating in agricultural studies from Cornell University. The charm and zeal in the young man sparked a flame of hope in him. Thus, in the year 1921, he formally invited Leonard Elmhirst to come to India from England and lead the 'Sriniketan Institute of Rural Reconstruction'. Yes, Elmhirst was a man who was to become his comrade in his dream endeavours and much more.

His silent message was... *Educate the villagers in self-reliance. And bring back life in its completeness to the villages with music and readings from the epics, as in the past.*

It was an epic effort that was destined to become historic.

Owing to his frustration during the Swadeshi Movement for not being taken very seriously and for being misinterpreted on various occasions, Rabindranath sought his retribution in his dream of self-reliance for a handful of his oppressed countrymen. In his mind, he knew that he couldn't help each and every one. The national leaders failed to understand his vision at that time. But he was certain that he could help a few families with his personal endeavours.

His song said it all: 'Jodi tor daak shune keu na aase tobe ekla cholo re' (If nobody cares to come in answer to thy call, walk alone).

It is hard to imagine a life as cheerless as that in our rural areas. I could hardly see a way out. It is not easy to do something for people who have cultivated weakness for centuries and don't know what self-help is. But I had to, anyhow, make a start...he said, during Visva Bharati Sammelani in the year 1922.

The years preceding the decade of the 1920s were perhaps the most difficult ones for the bard, who had gained global acclaim. In the year 1919, his youngest daughter, Mira, was at the pinnacle of an unhappy marriage, and Rabindranath finally threw away all social inhibitions.

So, when Mira left her husband's household, he

advised her not to return. His message was clear... '*I will not let her burn alive inside a circle of fire!*'

It was a year of great turmoil within the country, too, and Rabindranath couldn't tolerate the sheer brutality meted out to his countrymen. He returned the Nobel Prize on 31 May 1919, to protest against the Jallianwala Bagh massacre on 13 April.

Nonetheless, in his personal life, deep within his depression ate him like an army of termites. After the death of his wife and the assault of deathly hallows over his family and his children, he became like a vagabond in search of lost answers and a touch of peace. At a point, Rabindranath decided to seek refuge in establishing a connection with the other world. He performed planchette to know about his own future after the death of his wife, Mrinalini. It was the desperate struggle of a lonely soul to seek consolation from the supernatural.

Rabindranath had read *Human Personality and Its Survival After Death,* written by Myers. Mrinalini had been his invisible advisor whom he had failed to reciprocate with his love. But even via his planchette, he sought her counsel through the difficult tides of time. To her, in her memory, his words remained ingrained in his poems...

The time is past when I could repay for all I received
Her night has found its morning, and thou hast taken her to thy arms
And to thee I bring my gratitude and my gifts that were for her
For all hurts and offences to her, I come to thee for forgiveness.

I offer to thy service those flowers of my love that remained in bud
When she waited for them to open.

As a touch of spirituality calmed his distressed heart and mind, a persona of saintly tranquillity germinated within him. It helped him cross the river of grief and stand on the muddy shore of a new hope. Nevertheless, in his relentless creative efforts, the Rebellious Sun on his Golden Boat was blazing on with his furnace of global initiatives. The core was slowly withering with age. Around him, the fences of fire were slowly burning him to an ultimate zenith, but he knew that the pinnacle of every glory was always very lonely. Unloved in love and loved in through devotion, the bubbling Robi had metamorphosed into Gurudev.

Maybe only he knew what that soft heart within him dreamt for himself and for his countrymen. In a dream for freedom, he also dreamt of the liberation of the individual soul. The riddles playing ruckus in his heart got reflected within his lines when he wrote...

Where the mind is without fear and the head is held high;
Where knowledge is free;
Where the world has not been broken up into fragments by narrow domestic walls;
Where words come out from the depth of truth;
Where tireless striving stretches its arms towards perfection;
Where the clear stream of reason has not lost its way into the dreary desert sand of dead habit;
Where the mind is led forward by thee into ever-widening thought and action—
Into that heaven of freedom, my Father let my country awake.

Hence, as the new decade commenced, the journey of the bard, the educationalist, the universal citizen, continued across the globe. He became the *yatri,* a vagabond soul in the body of the stalwart poet in search of eternal peace and happiness.

Nevertheless, unnoticed by any, something else, a gust of freshness that would become an intimate source of energy for his own personal life, was about to touch him…soon.

Flashback—
Another Life in Another Continent:
'Victoria Ocampo, a soul of broken melodies…

Ramona Victoria Epifanía Rufina Ocampo was the oldest daughter of six, born to a wealthy family that had their roots in Argentina's feudal era. She was educated at home by her French governess. In a conservative society, she never received formal schooling. Her old, traditional, wealthy family frowned on formal education for women. But, amid the old-fashioned world that surrounded her, she was like an awry tempest. As she grew up, she began to blossom like a fragrant flower.

She later wrote: '*The alphabet-book in which I learned to read was French, as was the hand that taught me to draw those first letters…*'

Victoria was a rebel in her own way. Her dusky beauty and her vibrant personality created ripples in the hearts of the young men. The suitors roaming across the streets of Buenos Aires often dreamt of becoming her *Novio* whenever she stood upon the balcony.

Her eyes spoke with her heart: '*The man of your dreams would come like a tornado to sweep you away. You are a rebellious nymph who would give bliss to that tornado.'*

The tornado did come, and she got married in the year 1912. But the tornado played ruckus and shattered the chords of harmony!

Year 1914:
675 Tucuman Street. Buenos Aires, Argentina.

Victoria Ocampo sat upon the lone couch in her living room while tears rolled down her face profusely. In the last two years, her marriage to Bernando de Estrada (also known as Monaco Estrada) had been a disaster.

'The relationship has been a complete failure,' she sighed. 'We are both groping to find a way out of the dark tunnel. Failure to come out of this abysmal prison would finally kill us.'

She remembered her own words that she had inflicted upon Estrada the previous night. 'It is time for us to part ways. Leave me! Yes, leave me and liberate me from this prison... Liberate yourself from this prison!'

Sitting alone in the living room, her muffled sobs reverberated like the voice of an uncanny apparition. 'I must keep this façade... I cannot malign my family or my parents. This caged life is perpetual with a man who is devoid of all sentiments and romances.'

Her mind floated back to the days of her marriage with Estrada...

She was like a wild deer who dreamt of being lost in the woods, but he was too unromantic. Alas, she could only see that when it was too late. She had asked him that night, 'Where are we going? I want to go far away for the honeymoon. I want to be in some place that is miles and miles away.'

Estrada replied, 'Such a place would be too unfamiliar;

and the risks are higher. Let us go to Rome. I have made all the arrangements.'

The decision shattered her heart, and it was the defining moment when she understood that her hasty courtship with her Novio, followed by an even hasty marriage, was a wrong choice.

Despite so, Victoria continued to remain silent to keep the bonds of the relationship unbroken. They travelled to Europe and then to Rome, where her ravishing beauty, coupled with her sharp intelligence, won her accolades and the hearts of men. Her slim body, her vibrant complexion and the texture of her muslin-like skin converted her into a demigod in their eyes. It was the commencement of an era that was destined to win her perpetual admirations. Victoria felt special in those glances. It was a sentiment that she failed to grasp in the eyes of her own husband. But the conservative Estrada felt the pangs of jealousy as he witnessed everything. Their conjugal unions failed to touch her core, and the nights started to become darker. The alienation of hearts became harmonious with the union of their bodies, and thus the gap grew larger and larger.

Then, after another two years of failed struggles, Victoria Ocampo had begun a long-lasting affair with her husband's cousin Julián Martínez, a diplomat. It was a relationship that quenched her passionate inner desires. It was in Rome that she had first met Julián, and his intoxicating eyes kissed her eyes, as if his lips were kissing hers. Something clicked that night, and soon the episodes of romantic rendezvous began, after Victoria returned to Buenos Aires…

When her trance broke, her inner strength suddenly slipped off like a cloak, and she fell upon her knees, on the carpet, and cried profusely.

As the daylight faded completely, she went out for a walk along the footpath by the streets. The wind was again blowing awry. She walked alone among the crowd and then stood in front of a bookshop. On the shelf, she noticed a book. It was a French translation of a book of poems by an Indian poet named Rabindranath Tagore. A year ago, the man had won the Nobel Prize for Literature. She went inside and picked out the slim book. It was named *Gitanjali.* The name meant 'An Offering of Songs' and it had been translated by Andre Gide. With a little curiosity and a mechanical spark in her heart, she purchased the book and went back to her apartment.

That night, she stood by the window of her bedroom, against the chimney of white-marble, and read the verses. In the flooding moonlight, the lines written by the unknown poet from a distant land touched her to the core! Perhaps, neither the stony heart of Estrada nor the passionate love of Martínez had ever reached the depths of that core in Victoria Ocampo.

She sighed, 'Oh no…this is touching my heart at a point where nobody could ever reach...'

Thou hast made me endless, such is thy pleasure;
This frail vessel thou emptiest again and again;
And fillest it ever with fresh life…

The lines were like a fragrant perfume that overwhelmed her senses. Victoria read on and on…

Thy infinite gifts come to me only on these very small hands of mine.
Ages pass, and still thou purest, and still there is room to fill.

Now it is time to sit quiet, face to face with thee.
And to sing dedication of life in this silent and overwhelming leisure.

Victoria's eyes became moist in tears as the lines continued to penetrate her blood...

Have you heard his silent steps?
He comes, comes and ever comes.
Every moment and every age, every day and every night,
He comes, comes and ever comes.

His words brought infinite solace to the distraught Victoria, and she smiled in the mild moonlight. The invisible and the unknown poet, Rabindranath, won her heart like no other.

That night, she perhaps fell in love...a true love.

'Oh, unknown poet from across the oceans, how could you fathom the depths of my heart and read the invisible wounds within me?' she asked the winds.

There was nobody to answer her. Perhaps it was destiny's wish that she would have to wait for years before she could hear his voice.

In her personal life, the struggle she had embarked upon was a complex one. The social ties were like chains that dragged her down while she writhed in pain to set herself free. Yet, she had voluntarily chosen to remain a captive while her estranged husband continued to pierce her heart to bleed invisibly. Julián Martínez continued to provide her the solace of an elusive partner.

Then, five more years later, Victoria's father passed away. She had pledged to keep her father's name untainted. Hence, during his lifetime, she kept quiet about the storm in her marital relationship. Another year after his death, she formally separated from Estrada.

Was Victoria Ocampo truly happy with Julián Martínez?
Did her final independence bring her solace?
Did she, at last, get to discover the real definition of love?...

None but she knew the answers. Or, maybe not.

Year 1924: Rabindranath's visit to China and Japan.

Rabindranath aspired to welcome scholars from other countries to Visva Bharati, the educational institution at Santiniketan. With the funds donated by Jugal Kishore Birla, he embarked upon a journey to China in 1924. 'The Lecture Association of Peking' invited him, and he welcomed the invitation with the hopes that it would strengthen the ties between the two countries and enrich Visva Bharati through the cultural association.

Accompanied by Kshitihmohan Sen (of Visva Bharati's Indology Department), Nandalal Bose (of Kala Bhavan) and Leonard Elmhirst, they set out on board the SS *Ethiopia* on 24 March 1924. He stayed in China for just under seven weeks and was able to successfully deliver more than two dozen lectures. He delivered his lectures in Shanghai, Peking and five of China's twenty-four provincial capitals: Hangchow, Nanking, Tsinan, Taiyuan and Wuchang.

As he sailed along the Yangtze River, while travelling to Nanking from Shanghai, the natural bounty of China created a spiritual elation within him. The solitary 'yatri', the lone traveller, felt solace in that beauty, while his mission united with a greater vision of compassion and harmony of mankind.

That night, as he stood on the boat's deck, the dark canopy of the night was studded with the multitude of twinkling stars. The thatched cottages along the banks became alive with the flickering earthen lamps within their cores. The colossal hills, standing afar like the gigantic dragons, were surrounded by an aura of mist.

Rabindranath took a deep breath and sighed a melancholic sigh, '*The beauty in these nightly canvases reminds me of the time when I was a young, restless zamindar! Life was different then. And life is different now. But both have enriched me in their own contrasting romances and tragedies.*'

Then, the next morning, when the glowing sunlight illuminated everything, he saw the fleet of boats with their sails stretched high in the air, and he again sighed. But this was a sigh of confidence, '*I feel that my own sail had caught the wind. It is carrying me from my captivity, from the sleeping past and is bringing me out into the new world.*'

Despite the overall success of his lectures, he faced some resistance from the Chinese youth, who challenged his views about the greatness of the ancient Chinese civilization. After his second lecture at Peking, they expressed... *Since he has come to indoctrinate us, we must express the displeasure his lectures create in us.*

From China, he sailed to Japan on 30 May 1924 and stayed there for four weeks. As a global citizen and a bard of world literature, Rabindranath was now an acclaimed figure whose dream institution at Santiniketan bloomed under his tutelage among a diversity of pupils from across the world.

On his return from China and Japan, Rabindranath

hardly spent two months in his abode before he again embarked upon another journey that was destined to remain etched in his own memory. Leonard Elmirst, now a close aide and confidante, was again his companion in this journey. Rabindranath was sixty-three years old with delicate health, yet the vibrancies in his persona carried a charm of spring.

Year 1924: The unanticipated halt in Argentina...

Upon the invitation from the government of the Republic of Peru, he went on a voyage to visit Peru. Doctors advised him against a railroad journey through the mountains; thus, his trip was planned via Buenos Aires in Argentina. A special arrangement was made for his comfortable travel, even though deep within he remained lonely. The burden of extraordinary fame created a pinnacle, on top of which he remained a solitary soul.

In his long journey across the ocean, he spent most of the time sleeping and the rest of the time reading. However, the sense of attainment made him feel scared within his heart. He felt nervous about the welcome of an official 'Reception Committee'. In his thoughts, the vagabond within him escaped towards an unknown destination, but his heart desired the solace where he could be truly himself.

In September 1924, the news about his passage through Buenos Aires had already made headlines, and Victoria Ocampo, the now accomplished Argentine writer and literary activist (who worked for the famous daily *La Nacion*), felt overjoyed about the prospect of meeting him. His works had left her captivated, and she was too eager to meet him.

Alas, during this trip, he fell seriously ill and had to take an urgent halt in Buenos Aires to recuperate from his ailment. He was housed at the 'Hotel Plaza'. Victoria was pained by the sudden ailment of Rabindranath, but her heart trembled with excitement about another thought.

That evening, when he arrived at the hotel, Victoria was near the 'Plaza San Martín' with her friend Adelia Acevedo. Rabindranath was down with acute influenza and was under strict medical supervision. Victoria was unable to resist the temptation and said, 'Let's go. I must meet him tonight.'

As they reached the hotel, the buzz was loud that the illustrious poet was severely ill and no visitors were allowed to meet him. As Victoria and her friend stood with a morose countenance, a tall Englishman with blonde hair came and met them. He was Leonard Elmhirst.

Elmhirst greeted them and said, 'He is seriously indisposed with influenza. The doctor has visited him and says that his heart is quite weak. He has advised strict rest for Tagore. He concluded that the poet is in no condition to take the strains of further travel unless he recovers. Alas, we would have to cancel the trip to Peru. I shall write to the President and seek an apology.'

With a sudden gush of an unknown impulse, Victoria Ocampo uttered, 'I would be honoured and glad to host him at our country house in San Isidro! Please, sir, please do not refuse. I assure you that he can stay there for an indefinite period unless his health fully recovers. I promise, I will personally take care of him...'

Something sparked in the eyes of Elmhirst, and a smile surfaced across his lips. Perhaps the assurance in her words or the confidence in her striking beauty convinced him and silenced all his doubts.

He replied, 'Thank you. Please come with me. I will take you to his room. You can meet him personally. But please make it brief.'

The response was like a bolt of thunder, and Victoria froze for a moment. That much-sought-after time had arrived. Escorted by Elmhirst, she and her friend went up the hotel's corridor and then entered the room.

Within the sprawling room, they waited with bated breath. Then, dressed in his customary robe, Rabindranath slowly walked in. His beard was white, and his frail body at sixty-three years of age was visibly weak. Yet, his tall frame, his sparkling eyes and his ever-luminous smile stole away Victoria's heart. Yes, once again it was magic! Despite the onslaught of age, his skin seemed to her like a shining muslin and his persona was like that of a young prince from across the seven seas. His voice, though down with his ailment, sounded like the sweet masculine melody of a flute.

As her friend chattered nonstop with the bard, Victoria stood like a stone statue, with her eyes fixed upon his. Something sparkled in those pairs of eyes that night, both his and hers, and created a bond of a lifetime.

Finally, Victoria Ocampo offered him her cordial hospitality and added, 'I would not let you refuse my earnest request. You must come. I promise to devote myself to your service. I would not let go of this opportunity to be with you, whose words could heal me from the other side of the globe. Now, I must do my little bit to heal your health. The world needs you, and I want to be a small part of that journey.'

Rabindranath listened to her words and stood silent for a minute. Then he smiled, held her hands softly, and replied, 'Yes, Ms Ocampo, I will come...'

He moved his hands rhythmically and orated a few lines and then laughed heartily. Perhaps he laughed like a child after a long time.

When Rabindranath was suffering and was in severe pain in Buenos Aires, Victoria met him with a warmth that had the touch of an ethereal love. It won his heart immediately. When she made arrangements for him to rest and recover in her villa at San Isidro, on the banks of Río de la Plata (commonly referred to in English as River Plate), his consent was natural.

Thus, the bard was again ushered into a world whose reminiscences were preordained to become perpetual. Many questions surrounded his decision, but he chose to answer none of them. It was his life and his choice.

Thus, none had the authority to question him... '*Was it not a voluntary choice to be in the solitary company of a mystic woman who admired him deeply? Was it the desperate striving of the bard to live a life of romance, once more? Was the cherub within his heart trying to bring in the throbbing joys of youth into his ageing body?*'

Rabindranath thus became the coveted companion of Victoria Ocampo.

Puravi—The Sweet Twilight

'Someday I shall sing to thee in the sunrise of some other world, I have seen thee before in the light of the earth, in the love of man...'

Rabindranath's travel to Buenos Aires and his time with Victoria Ocampo brought back a youthful vigour within him. A visibly ill Tagore shifted to Villa Miralrío near Villa Ocampo at the behest of Victoria Ocampo. A gust of energy swept into his life, even though the time was short-lived. The sixty-three-year-old was perhaps destined to share a wonderful bond of love with her that was beyond the cages of time and age.

Early November 1924: Buenos Aires.

Victoria approached her family to make Villa Ocampo available for a week to host Rabindranath. However, the ever-conservative reply from the family was a 'no'.

Victoria was heartbroken, but she didn't want to lose the opportunity that destiny had given her. She hurried to meet a relative, named Ricardo de Lafuente Machain. To him she urged, 'Please allow me to rent the Villa Miralrío for a week. The San Isidro country house would host the illustrious poet Rabindranath Tagore from India. Please do not refuse this request.'

The heartfelt request was accepted, and thus, Victoria plunged all her energies into making the place ready for her enchanted guest. With the speed of light, she arranged a facelift of the place. Built in the style of a Spanish villa with a sprawling garden that boasted a beautiful garden of flowers and a gorgeous tipa tree. The balcony lent a fantastic view of the Río de la Plata. Villa Miralrío had just been completed, and Ocampo thought it was the best abode for Rabindranath.

She arranged for a cook and a houseboy and also sent her omnipresent nurse, Fani, to take care of her coveted guest. The latter had an all-encompassing influence around Victoria that was to the limit of a dictatorial nanny who was overprotective of Victoria.

Middle of November 1924: Villa Miralrío, San Isidro.

Victoria drove down Rabindranath and Elmhirst (now a voluntary secretary to him) to the picturesque suburb of San Isidro. As Rabindranath and Elmhirst sat in the car, she drove the car. As the beauty of the Argentinian summer unfolded with her beauty of natural bounty, she could get a glimpse of the slow sunrise of a youthful ecstasy in the face of the bard. The sun was playing a mischievous game of hide and seek with the clouds, and he seemed to thoroughly enjoy the mischief with a childlike pleasure.

The car reached the campus of Villa Miralrío, and they entered the beautiful abode alongside the river. The first glance of the exquisite garden, the limitless colours of the flowers within it and the bountiful tipa tree made him feel an exquisite happiness.

As the winds whistled through the foliage of the green

leaves of the tall trees and dwarf bushes, Rabindranath laughed and said to his companions, 'Look, they are giggling like little children. I wish I could understand their jokes and could giggle with them!'

The three of them went up the stairs and reached the first floor. Two rooms, adjacent one, had been allocated to Rabindranath and Elmhirst. Victoria ushered them inside and stared at Rabindranath. The changing colours in that expressive face were like the changing seasons.

For a moment, Victoria felt as if Rabindranath was like a young lover, in front of whose eyes was his muse dressed in exotic floral attire and was trying to woo him passionately. It was like a call wherein the heroine was summoning her hero for a much-coveted union. And the hero, overwhelmed and intoxicated by her beauty, was running behind his muse.

Rabindranath walked inside and then slowly went out onto the balcony. Outside, the gorgeous view of the river drew in a sensation of limitlessness. Rabindranath was thrilled. He swirled like a child, gyrating slowly and peacefully in his long robe, and added with a hearty smile, 'This is what I believe is the true meaning of freedom. In this overindulgence of beauty, my market value can be obscured by my personal value. Here, every touch of nature brings in a touch of life!'

The moments on the balcony were like a final moment of that romance when the hero held his heroine in his arms, and the beautiful union began to unfold.

Victoria introduced Fani, the houseboy and the other servants to the guests and said, 'I shall spend the nights in my family-owned Villa Ocampo. It is just a few blocks away. I hope your stay here is comfortable and your health recovers soon.'

Under the care and hospitality of the talented and charming lady, he was destined to rejuvenate not only his falling health but also his lost love in his own very existence.

The sun was setting in that beautiful South American summer opera. Rabindranath took a deep breath and sat down. Dinner was getting ready and was soon served to the illustrious guest.

That night, as Victoria Ocampo went back to the Villa Ocampo, a subtle thought began to germinate in her mind. She couldn't fathom what it was, but she understood that it was a soft touch of a cocktail of love and devotion. The true answer was still hidden behind a mist.

She took out the letter that Rabindranath had written to her and read it quietly. The words were like drops of dew that touched her heart, and she felt happy.

November–December 1924: San Isidro. One Week Later and Then on...

The seven days passed by too soon, but the days left their lasting impact on the hearts of both Rabindranath and Victoria. For that week that went like a tempest, she dedicated herself to taking care of him while soaking her own soul in the light of the *Rebellious Sun*.

The next morning, Victoria arrived to greet her illustrious guest. Her cook and her servants were busy with their arrangements for breakfast. Rabindranath was not inside his room. Victoria came out of the villa and went into the garden. As she walked up a few paces, she saw him standing at a distance, under the tipa tree.

Victoria quietly went and stood beside him. The breeze was cool and soothing. He looked at her and smiled back. She greeted him, 'Good morning...'

Rabindranath greeted back and then stared at the exquisite foliage of the tree and was soon lost in a tranquil world. Without moving his glance, he said softly, 'Have you read my letter? It was not a thank-you note. It is my heartfelt confession.'

'Yes, I have read it,' replied Victoria.

Rabindranath continued, 'It is true that as my market price has risen, my own personal value has become obscured. At the zenith of fame, I feel the loneliest. I have become a deity and have ceased to be the human I always wanted to be. My heart really ached to break away from the shrine where I had been imprisoned, to become a mortal again. What I wrote to you is raw but true. What I told you in my first letter is very correct. The touch of human emotion can only come from a woman's love, and I have been hoping for a long time that I deserve it. Your invitation and this stay give me that rare opportunity...'

As he spoke, Victoria softly held his hands. His frail fingers quivered as her fingers touched his. Then she held his arms and said with a smile, 'Come, let us go inside. Breakfast is ready. Let us begin a new episode today.'

Inside the house, at the breakfast table, Elmhirst greeted them. The young man was visibly in awe of the subtle beauty of Victoria. The glitter in his eyes spoke out his heart, even though his lips were silent. Despite his weak health and progressing age, Rabindranath's youthful heart didn't fail to notice it.

Fani was busy serving the food with the help of the servants. However, a barrier in their language created a comical episode as she tried to converse with Rabindranath. The latter was prolific and used a dramatic sign of his fingers to ask her to get him what he wanted. As everyone broke into a fit of laughter, he took a piece of paper to draw a cup of coffee that he wanted, and Fani got him a cup of hot tea with a wide grin on her face!

Thus, the day proceeded while Victoria sat with him and the two spoke with each other. Rabindranath was still very weak and needed an ample amount of rest.

Elmhirst suggested, 'You must not engage yourself in your literary pursuits right away. I suggest that you recover some more before you get down to work. I have notified the authorities about the situation, and your trip to Peru has been cancelled. You need an ample amount of recovery to become fully fit.'

Like an obedient child, Rabindranath agreed. Victoria sat with him and spoke her heart out. He listened to her words, in her broken English expression, and smiled. He understood her, despite knowing her for such a limited time.

One day melted into another, and soon the week passed. The doctor visited Villa Miralrío and suggested that Rabindranath needed more time before he could be ready to travel again.

Victoria understood that she had to do something drastic so that his stay could remain uninterrupted. She was desperate to keep him nestled within her own aura.

That night, she went into her bedroom at Villa Ocampo and opened the locked cabinet. In the darkness of the night, she took out something that glittered in the mild moonlight that was peeping in through her window. It was her prized crescent-shaped diamond tiara.

Victoria held it near her bosom, looked into the mirror on the wall and smiled, 'Tonight, somebody has become more precious than you. Tonight and beyond, your value is insignificant in comparison to him.'

Victoria sold off the tiara and went to visit Ricardo de Lafuente Machain. She sat down in front of him with a determined demeanour and said, 'I want to rent our Villa Miralrío for the rest of the summer. Please do not refuse. I seriously need your help, and I am ready to pay for it.'

Thus, at ten thousand pesos, the Villa Miralrío got rented and Victoria Ocampo was content with what her heart truly desired. Then, she headed out towards the furniture shop.

Two days later, early in the morning, Victoria arrived at Villa Miralrío with a huge parcel. The object got delivered upstairs, on the balcony of the room on the first floor. It was the room that had been allocated to Rabindranath. The latter was away for a walk in the garden. As the task of delivery was complete, Victoria sat in a corner of the room and waited.

Within the next fifteen minutes, Rabindranath arrived. He still walked slowly, and he still looked weak. But a glitter had come in the pupils of his eyes. Victoria felt happy as she noticed it. She looked at him from behind a curtain as the bard walked inside his room. Then, she stepped out quietly and held her palms over his eyes.

Rabindranath held her hands and smiled. Victoria said, 'Today, I am so happy. Today, the happiness in your eyes makes me feel content. I knew from your writings that you love the proximity to Mother Nature and her serenity. The peaceful expression on your face tells me that I was not wrong. Now come with me, I want to show you something...'

With his eyes blindfolded by the soft hands of Victoria, Rabindranath walked on. As they reached the balcony, the cool breeze from the Río de la Plata touched them with a silken softness. Victoria removed her hands, and Rabindranath opened his eyes. In front of him, placed tranquilly upon the balcony, was a beautiful wooden armchair. The very look of the exquisite chair carried a subtle charm of tranquillity. Victoria held his arms and made him sit down upon it. Rabindranath sat down and rested upon it. He felt at peace, and a smile came upon his face.

Victoria sat down near his feet, and Rabindranath touched her palms softly. He closed his eyes and said, 'The simple elegance of this balcony mingled with the comfort of this chair and the charm of the eloquent view of the river is just priceless! This is the best gift I have received in many years. This is a love that I shall never forget till my last breath and perhaps beyond that too.'

Victoria felt ecstatic. She sat quietly and looked into his eyes. He added, 'Victoria, my dear, a huge barrier of language and spoken conversation floats between us. But, today, I want to present you with a name in my own language, in Bengali...'

'What is it, Gurudev?' she asked. He was like the sage of love, the Cupid of eternity, who held the magic wand to heal all her pains and overwhelm her heart with true love. He was like her master, her Guru.

'Vijaya.' replied Rabindranath. 'I want to gift you this name. In Bengali, *Vijaya* means "The Victorious Princess", or in other words, it means Victoria!'

Victoria stood up and hugged him. The sudden charge of emotion was abrupt, and Rabindranath felt the electrifying touch of her affection. She repeated his words, 'Vijaya… My new name, my new identity is Vijaya ... I shall prize this name till the last day of my life.'

Rabindranath smiled at her and said, 'In Bengali, the language that blooms in my blood, this pure bond of love is called *bhalobasha.* I am glad that it is able to connect us so deeply.'

The gorgeous morning, soaked in the innocence of a budding love beyond the barriers of language and continents, merged the two hearts in a pure attachment.

The armchair was not just an innate piece of decorated furniture. It became a companion for the dreary bard whose heart craved for a drop of love.

Glimpses of another fond day came back to him as a beautiful vision. It was a day that was lost decades ago along the shores of the Arabian Sea. It was a day when a young Robi stood inside his room at the bungalow of Dr Atmaram. That day, as Robi had entered his room, he saw the huge English-style window overlooking the seashore. Robi had stood spellbound in front of the window. As he had opened the glass windows, the salty wind gusted in and splashed upon his face, as if it was trying to tell him… '*Taste the sweet honey of youth. Robi, she is the goddess of your youthful fantasy! There is nothing right or wrong in life. Perhaps this awry wind of romance will redefine your soul.*'

Rabindranath made a meticulous routine while he stayed in San Isidro. His day was divided into a few activities that helped him recuperate. Early in the morning, he woke up and sat down to write. He had requested complete privacy during those few hours. He often sat upon the armchair and immersed himself in his poetic waves while the new dawn unfolded. It was as if *the New Dawn was greeting the Rebellious Sun.*

If he was not in the armchair, he sat by the writing desk and wrote his heart out. Then, he went out in the garden for a quiet stroll amid the blossoms or a few tranquil minutes under the serenity of the tipa tree.

On one such morning, he stood under the shade of the tipa tree and looked at the garden. A few blossoms had withered while a few buds had arrived. A few colourful flowers were in full bloom. The entire atmosphere created a vibrant sentiment everywhere.

He looked at them quietly as flashes of the yesteryears went past his eyes. Inside, his inner voice—that had been silent for a long time—again spoke with him. It said, '*Gone are the days of childish frivolity. Gone are the days of youthful disobedience. Gone are the people who ignited the flames of love in you. Gone are those who wrote new meanings of love in your heart. Yet, as the evening nears, and we stand at the shore of the Latin American river, the Rebellious Sun, once again, meets the placid Moon, perhaps for one last time.*'

Then, he walked out through the gates of Villa Miralrío, into the street. His strength had returned a bit, and he headed down the road to reach Villa Ocampo. Victoria was in her living room. She rushed out and received him. It was a moment of happiness as she saw that her Gurudev was again becoming stronger.

The two of them sat in the solitude within Villa Ocampo and spoke with each other. For hours, there were none to interrupt them. Despite subtle hindrances to vocal expressions, they understood each other.

Victoria held the story of her life like an open book in front of Rabindranath while the latter listened to her patiently. Even though she refrained from disclosing her relationship with Julián Martínez, her honest confession intensified their bond. None saw or heard them that morning as it melted away into the afternoon.

Rabindranath kissed her on her forehead, and she closed her eyes to absorb that untamed affection. Then, Rabindranath said, 'Vijaya, do you know how we have become so close to each other within such a little time? It is because there are so many similarities and so many dissimilarities that are complementary in the two of us.'

She looked at him quietly, while he continued. 'We were both born in an aristocratic milieu, into a tightly knit clan of social reformers who held deep conservative values. We were both educated at home, and we both shared a strong passion for the expression of freedom. We were both exposed to the European culture during our late teens and early twenties, and we got to taste something new. We have both faced the upheavals of emotions and the turmoil of relationships. Yet, we are different in our beliefs about independence and the way in which we look at the outer world. You wanted to become an actress, and I wanted to pursue literature. But we were both restricted from striving for those dreams and were deemed redundant in the social strata we belonged to. We were both in search of a peace that kept on behaving like an elusive nymph. Our cuisine is different, just like our languages are. However, within such a kaleidoscopic drama playing ruckus in our lives, a touch of innocent love connected us. Today, a gaping hollow of three decades separates us. Yet, the fragrance of purity unites us.'

That afternoon, they walked back to Villa Miralrío for lunch. She held his arms, as if trying to soak in the deep spiritual sensation that haloed his heart.

It was in Villa Miralrío where Rabindranath composed some of the finest poems which were to entice the victorious princess, Vijaya. In his affection and attachment toward her, Rabindranath had presented her with the name Vijaya. It was a name that she had secretly determined to use lovingly for the rest of her life!

With a rejuvenated heart, he wrote many wonderful poems during his stay and even dedicated some to his beloved Vijaya. That night, as he again sat upon the armchair and looked at the night sky, he took his notebook and scribbled down a poem…

'Atithi' (Guest)

Woman, thou hast made my days of exile
Tender with beauty,
And has accepted me to thy nearness
With a simple grace
That is like the smile with which the
Unknown star welcomed me
When I stood alone on the balcony and
Gazed upon the southern night.

Then came the voice from above: 'We
Know you,

For you came as our guest from the dark of
The infinite, the guest of light.'
Even in the same great voice thou hast
Cried to me: 'I know you'
And though I know not thy tongue,
Woman, I have heard it uttered in
Thy music—
'You are ever our guest on this earth,
poet, the guest of love.'

A stark barrier remained in the mode of communication between the two. Within her comfortable hospitality, a beautiful relationship developed between them. The only European language that Rabindranath was proficient in was English. However, a less competent Victoria sometimes struggled with her expressions in the same language. Yet, despite the shortcomings of a spoken expression, the bond of love continued to deepen.

She sat beside him one morning and said, 'Gurudev, this piece of paper on your lap is empty. Why don't you sketch something? Why don't you express your creative self in a visual form? I insist that you do. The world must know how you see the characters that you create. We deserve to see how you look at the world with your own eyes.'

Thus, he took up the pencil and drew the sketches. Victoria went away to finish a pending work, but he sat on his armchair and did something drastic. Hours went by, and he finished something on two separate pages. He sat quietly for a few moments and laughed heartily. Victoria and Elmhirst rushed in to see what was going on.

As they arrived, they saw two pieces of paper. On one, there was the sketch of a bearded man with a strange frown. On the other, there was the oval female face with brooding eyes.

As they stood, Rabindranath smiled and said, 'These are my first sketches... Let me introduce you to Rabindranath and his Vijaya!'

Victoria Ocampo prided herself on the fact that she encouraged him in his manuscript doodling, from which his visual art eventually emerged. She said to him with ecstatic laughter, 'Gurudev, I, your Vijaya, have succeeded in doing something that many had failed to do. I have awakened a great painter within the soul of a great poet...'

On another afternoon, in December, as Rabindranath sat with Victoria under the tipa tree, he said, 'You know, I always believed that a true home is where a person's surroundings come together to churn out the best within him or her. In your company, Vijaya, the summer breeze has brought the same sense of fulfilment in me as I stay here at this villa in San Isidro. Despite the barriers of language, I think we are able to understand each other's sentiments without much difficulty.'

Then, they sat together in each other's company, played with words and tried to laugh away their best opportunities to understand each other clearly. He added, while they laughed, 'In our failure to fully comprehend what our verbal expressions are, we do succeed in touching our hearts.'

That afternoon, Rabindranath said to her passionately, 'I know how much you love me. It is a love that has germinated within a short span and invigorated me to accomplish the last purpose of my own life. This beautiful friendship, which got its genesis within our hearts, is ethereal. It has given me a final chance to taste the innocence of childhood and the honey of youth before my sunset arrives...'

He told her, while she sat and watched him, 'You are indeed the only one who has come to know me so closely when I am old and young at the same time.'

Victoria sighed within her heart, 'I am so close to you and yet utterly unhappy to know that you cannot be near me forever...'

Elmhirst was not only a voluntary secretary for Rabindranath but also a constant confidant and companion. He was already engaged to Dorothy, but the charm of Victoria Ocampo touched his heart, too. Despite the pangs of Cupid that drove him to play truant, he continued to play the role of a mediator of communications between Rabindranath and Victoria on many occasions. A beeline of visitors arrived every day to meet the illustrious poet, and the latter too enjoyed their company as he sat with them and spent hours, sometimes even under the tipa tree. Elmhirst and Victoria often felt angered because they were concerned about his health. However, the bard was experiencing a new springtime of youth, and none could stop him. His heart and his health became better and stronger with every passing day.

At times, Victoria felt irritated by the infatuation that Elmhirst harboured in himself towards her. However, she knew that he was young, and her own attraction was too strong to be ignored. The three, accompanied by Victoria's friend Adelia Acevedo, spent a week at Chapadmalal, near Mar del Plata, where a few poems were written by Rabindranath. The South American sojourn gave him his last taste of youthful fantasy, and the Rebellious Sun could sail valiantly upon his Golden Boat to create his literary masterpieces.

January 1925: Buenos Aires.

The two months floated away too soon. The fifty-eight days, to be more precise, went away like a gust of wind. Finally, it was time to say goodbye. A day before his departure, Rabindranath held her hands and said, 'Vijaya, I can never forget you...'

She replied, 'Why do you have to leave so fast? I am afraid you will never know how much I love you. Remember Gurudev, you have left here someone who is trying to find expression for her love for you.'

He added, 'That expression needs no form, my dear. It comes like a telepathic vibe from your soul to mine. Even though I leave, I will remain alive within you. So, from today, love yourself. Vijaya, there is so much to be done. There is so much you can do. The world is always your victorious journey. I want you to pursue that dream. It is a dream of the Rebellious Sun. You must explore it and write your own sojourn. Vijaya, you shall shine till eternity.'

On 3 January 1925, Rabindranath left Buenos Aires. Victoria booked two cabins onboard the Italian liner SS *Giuleo Cesaro* for him. One cabin was to be used as his bedroom, while the other was his study where he could write in comfort.

Victoria even arranged to send the armchair on

board the ship for him. The captain of the ship was hesitant, but she persuaded him with her constant banters to remove the door of the cabin so that the armchair could be placed inside.

When Rabindranath entered the cabin, he was pleasantly surprised. Victoria looked back at him and said, 'I hope you will be able to rest here when you feel tired.'

As they parted, Rabindranath whispered into her ears, '*Puravi,* the eastern winds have started to blow. Vijaya, I know that they would soon touch you in the same way they have touched me. Until the day we meet again, I will look forward to that moment...'

That day, the ship embarked upon a journey towards Italy, from where, after a brief stopover, the bard was to sail back to India. As he stood on the deck and said goodbye, drops of tears appeared near the brim of his eyes.

Far ashore stood Victoria as she waved her goodbye until the ship floated away deep within the brink of the horizon. She was both happy and sad. His words reverberated within her mind and brought a smile to her lips... '"*Sur*", *the melody hidden in the music of life is an ethereal gift. It cannot be heard with the ears. One must hear it in the silence of the heart. Yes, that is where love creates a symphony. It is in that peaceful music, where I found "Love" in you...*'

Victoria turned back to return. Her journey into the world of peace and harmony had just begun. She knew that Rabindranath had given her a passion. He had given a new reason to live for her own self. She sighed and smiled, '*Sur*...the music of life!'

Mayar Khela—The Play of Dreams

'Let me not beg for the stilling of my pain,
but for the heart to conquer it...'

Rabindranath stayed at San Isidro for one month and twenty days. The next year after his return, his book of poems was published and was titled *Puravi*. It was dedicated to Victoria Ocampo. When Rabindranath left, she got his favourite armchair shipped to go with him.

Rabindranath perhaps again metamorphosed into a young Robi, as he sat upon it and lived a heavenly dream. Throughout his return journey and even after, he wrote many letters to Victoria.

The power of their relationship, beyond every barrier of language and country, remained strong and beautiful. For the entire next year, and even beyond, the intensity of his voice reverberated through his letters from the very day he departed from Buenos Aires.

Letter dated 5 January 1925. Onboard the SS *Giuleo Cesaro*...

Vijaya,

Under a grey sky, my days are repeated in monotonous rhymes, like a perpetual telling of beads. I pass most of my day and a great part of my night deeply buried in your armchair, which, at last, has explained to me the lyrical meaning of the poem of Baudelaire that I read with you. I had hoped that I should be able to do some writing while crossing the interval between two shores, but the wind has veered and my manuscript book lies idle, its virgin pages looking like the sandy beach of a distant island unexplored. My day is divided into two-thirds of sleep and one-third of reading. I am surrounded by a deep atmosphere of laziness as befits a human male in an ideal condition of life. In these two days, I have been able to understand why Chinamen must smoke opium to realize intensely for a few moments the profound dignity of the male, his natural birthright of inutile passiveness of which he is forcibly deprived the rest of his waking hours... I only wish you could see how greatly Leonard has improved since he has got his leisure on this ship. He has suddenly turned an astronomer, hunting the upper deck, waiting for a chance of meeting some star of the first magnitude belonging to the southern hemisphere. You know, human males as secretaries are inefficient, but as astronomers, they know how to make their opportunities rich and shining. I suppose you know that, also for me, astronomy has a great attraction, but being a poet, I have my chart of stars in my memory, which I can study even when I am confined in my cabin. I have been advised never to joke with a woman, but I am afraid that some of the observations in this letter show signs of frivolity. You will excuse me when you know that a man who is not a prophet and yet who is treated as a prophet must give vent to his fit of laughter even at the risk of misunderstanding.

Portions of a letter dated 13 January 1925. Onboard the SS *Giuleo Cesaro*...

> *I am drifting farther and farther away from your shore, and now it has become possible for me to set the vision of my everyday surroundings at San Isidro against a background of separation. I am not a born traveller. I do not have the energy and strength needed to know a strange country and help the mind to gather materials from a wide area of new experiences for building its foreign nest. And therefore, when I am away from my own land, I seek for some individuals who may represent to me the country to which they belong. For me, the spirit of Latin America will ever dwell in my memory, incarnated in your person. You rescued me from the organized hospitality of a reception committee and allowed me to receive through yourself the personal touch of your country. Unfortunately, there was a barrier of language that prevented a free enough communication of minds between us, for you never felt fully at home in the only European language I happen to know. It was unfortunate because you have a richness of mind which naturally longs to offer its own tribute to those whom you accept as your friends, and I fully understand the pain which you must have suffered from not being able to reveal adequately to me your deeper thoughts and to dissolve the fog that screened off the world of your intellectual life from my vision. I am deeply sorry, it has not been possible for me to have an acquaintance of your complete personality, the difficulty having been enhanced owing to the literary character of your mind. For such a mind has its aristocratic code of honour about*

its manner of self-expression, choosing to remain dumb rather than to send out its thoughts dressed in rags.

...One thing most of my friends fail to know is that where I am real, I am profoundly serious. Our reality is like a treasure; it is not left exposed and only in the outer chamber of our personal self. It waits to be explored, and only in our serious moments can it be approached. You have often found me homesick; it was not so much for India; it was for that abiding reality in me in which I can have my inner freedom. It becomes totally obscured when, for some reason or other, my attention is too much directed upon my own personal self. My true home is there where from my surroundings comes the call to me to bring out the best that I have, for that inevitably leads me to the touch with the universal. My mind must have a nest to which the voice of the sky can descend freely, the sky that has no other allurements but light and freedom.

...I tell you all this because I know you love me. I trust my Providence. I feel certain—and I say this in all humility—that he has chosen me for some special mission of his own and not merely for the purpose of linking the endless chain of generation. Therefore, I believe that your love may, in some way, help me in my fulfilment. It will sound egoistic, only because the voice of our ego has the same masterful cry of insistence as the voice of that which infinitely surpasses it. I assure you that through me, a claim comes that is not mine. A child's claim upon its mother has a sublime origin—it is not a claim of an individual; it is that of humanity. Those who come on some special errand of God are like that child; if they ever attract love and service, it should

be for a higher end than merely their enjoyment. Not only love, but hurt and insults, neglects and rejection come to grind them into dust but to kindle their life into a brighter flame.

Your friendship has come to me unexpectedly. It will grow to its fullness of truth when you know and accept my real being and see clearly the deeper meaning of my life. I have lost most of my friends because they asked me for myself, and when I said I was not free to offer myself away, they thought I was proud. I have deeply suffered from this over and over again—and therefore I always feel nervous whenever a new gift of friendship comes my way. But I accept my destiny, and if you also have the courage to fully accept it, we shall ever remain friends.

Letter dated 17 January 1925. Onboard the SS *Giuleo Cesaro*...

Tomorrow we shall reach Barcelona and then Genoa. I am about to leave my easy chair in my cabin. The chair has been my real nest for these two weeks, giving me rest and privacy and a feeling that my happiness is of value to somebody. I do not know when it will be possible for me to write to you again, but I shall always remember you.

Farewell.

Letter dated January-end in 1925. From Italy...

Dear Vijaya,

The same old stupid joke of fate, I have fallen ill again

and am compelled to give up all my engagements and hasten home. It is a great pity, for I have been deeply touched by the genuine feeling of regard for me by the people of this country. I must come back to them and fulfil their expectation. Leonard is working with our friends here to find a suitable place for me. I shall be very happy indeed to have my European nest in this delightful country, which is so friendly to me. I am sure to visit Italy next September and October if everything is settled before that time. I remember you said you also would come to Europe at that time, so you will once again have me for your guest under your own roof. I am writing to you lying on the bed. I hope you will be able to decipher my scrawl. Leonard is sure to write to you a detailed description of my visit to Italy.

Letter dated 1 February 1925. From Venice...

I shall sail for India tomorrow. Leonard will arrange with our friends here a quiet place where I may spend some part of my year. I remember you wished to come to Europe sometime next autumn, therefore I decided to meet you here about the middle of September, remaining here till the third week of October. If you are compelled to change your plan, let me know it beforehand. Italy has been very gracious to me and I feel that the Italian sun and the warmth of the Italian heart will do me good.

Goodbye.

Letter dated 19 February 1925. From Bombay, India ...

I have just reached India. The tired feeling persists. The doctor in Venice strongly advised me to be very careful in spending the small remnant of my energy, and I already feel that India is sure to make an extravagant claim upon it and exhaust my resources sooner than it could be helped. I am seriously thinking of leaving for Europe next April and spending the hot months there. Elmhirst has left me for a sphere completely out of my reach. It will be difficult for me to find a companion equally helpful who can fill the gap. I shall cable to you if I can start for Europe this summer.

Have you decided, the money which I earn from my writings in the Nacion, to reach me through Elmhirst and not directly? The programme for myself, which I have in my mind, will to a certain extent depend upon this contribution, and therefore I am anxious to receive it regularly and without much circumlocution. For the first year, at least, in his married life, Elmhirst's mind is not likely to be in its normal state of sanity, and therefore he should not be burdened with any responsibility in which a third party is concerned. However, I should not trouble myself too much about this matter, knowing for certain that you will look after my interests and I can have an absolute trust in any arrangement you make for my sake.

I do not know how long a letter takes to reach you from India, but I do hope it will be before the time I start for Europe. If you do not receive any cable from me, know that I am prevented from sailing from India and that my departure for Europe has been postponed.

Though you may not get letters from me too often, be sure that I remember you with my bhalobasha.

I have some misgivings about the continuity of my relationship with La Nacion*—someday it may be felt* *as unnecessary—and in that case, please never force my writings upon them, trying to tie them to their promise. As for my own necessity, it is not at all important.*

Letter dated 4 March 1925. Santiniketan…

I am writing this, reclining on your armchair, which I am afraid will keep me within its enclosure much longer than I calculated. I am much worse than I was when you saw me, and I am certain it will not be possible for me to leave India before August. I have asked my son to cancel my passage this summer.

I am sending you some of my short stories, translations of which I hope will be acceptable for La Nacion. *If it is not, make any use you like, for they have not yet been published.*

I suppose you have, by this time, heard from Italian sources how cordially I was received there. This has been a further inducement for me to seek my European home somewhere in Italy. I hope Elmhirst has been successful in cho[o]sing a suitable place. Have you heard from him?

I must close my letter here—my body refuses to work.

Bhalobasha.

Letter dated 29 October 1925…

Dear Vijaya,

I do not like to talk about my illness, which has become a bore in its endless monotony. I am wearily waiting for the summer to come, when I shall make another attempt to visit Europe to get proper medical treatment.

I am sending you a Bengali book of poems which

I wish I could place in your hand personally. I have dedicated it to you, though you will never be able to know what it contains. A large number of poems in this book were written while I was in San Isidro. My readers who will understand these poems will never know who Vijaya is with whom they are associated. I hope this book will have the chance for a longer time with you than its author had.

Bhalobasha.

Thus, his letters to her, while he reluctantly returned home, remained glowing testimonies of their bond. The coveted visit to Italy in September–October of the year 1925 didn't happen. However, Rabindranath did visit Europe in the year 1926, but again, unfortunately, Victoria was unable to meet him. The turmoil in her own personal life was too heavy, and Victoria failed to meet her Gurudev.

The three years that ensued after Rabindranath's return from Argentina were mostly marked by a peculiar silence in Victoria Ocampo. Perhaps she was sorting out her own life in Buenos Aires. Perhaps her silence was the reflection of an inner turmoil that she sought to erase. Perhaps it was a lasting impact of the bard that took her into a whirlwind.

Awkwardly, in her silence, she remained eternally mysterious, and Rabindranath plunged himself into a tsunami of creative activities. The manuscript doodling that he had taken up while in the company of Victoria became a means of his expression. At almost seventy years of age, he immersed himself in the world of painting.

After the culmination of the *Puravi* poems, his despondence with the saddest thoughts of love and death made him create yet more masterpieces...

Sitting inside his room, amid the abundance of canvases and paintbrushes, he murmured, '*In you, I can see the apparitions of a non-deliberate origin. In these swooshes, I can paint my deepest expression hidden behind the colours.*'

In his poem, he had written what his heart felt. He opened his notebook and read it out aloud. In that empty, behind the closed door, his voice echoed and spoke with him like an invisible companion...

Hark, where in the formless limbs, ghosts of sights and weeping haunt the night...
A time was when they had a form and a voice...
The fruitless sorrow of that has been and is now nameless, amorphous, unremembered,
Haunt the dim recesses of my mind, seeking a form a shelter.

Among about twelve self-portraits, by coloured doodles on a black-and-white photograph of himself, he created the image of a woman and another of an undetermined gender. Perhaps it was the expression of the harmony of the masculine and feminine that he expressed through his elusive creativity and chuckled within his own mind. He looked at the picture and commented, '*The picture has about it a sense of brooding melancholy—don't you notice it! Most of my pictures are like that—they lack laughter. I do not know why this should be so when I like a good laugh myself and love to make others laugh. Perhaps I have a touch of sadness—deep down.*'

Until the early part of the year 1926, he was hopeful about meeting Victoria once more in Europe. Regrettably, she didn't go to meet him. In the strange touch of love that the ageing bard had discovered, his suffering was what he gained once again.

What was the reason behind the silence of Victoria? None knew. Yet, the Bard in Love became immortalized in his own true and unblemished love and his creations.

Heartbroken by the jolt of destiny, Rabindranath took consolation in the company of the charming Rani Mahalanobis and plunged himself into a grand European tour.

Flashback—
A new association a few years ago...

Guru Charan Mahalanobis was a self-educated and first-generation businessman who had migrated to Calcutta from East Bengal in the previous century. He had established three educational institutions in Calcutta, namely the Brahmo Boys' School, the Brahmo Girls' School and the City School. His son, Prabodh Chandra Mahalanobis, went on to study arts and painting at the Art School of Calcutta, where he became acquainted with Upendranath Sircar, whose daughter Nirodbasini he later married. Together with his brother-in-law, the acclaimed doctor Nilratan Sircar, he established a dealership called *Carr and Mahalanobis*, which specialized in sports equipment and gramophones. Again, the business venture flourished across the country and brought fame and wealth to the family.

Prabodh Chandra's son was a brilliant young man

named Prasanta Mahalanobis. He was the eldest among his siblings and was educated at the Brahmo Boys' School. Despite the loss of his mother when he was just a teen, Prasanta went on to become a highly educated mathematician and statistician. After World War I, he stayed in India and joined as a temporary Assistant Professor at the physics department of Presidency College, Calcutta. Soon, he went on to become a professor.

Prasanta, the man who would later found the Indian Statistical Institute, became a young professor who was very close to Rabindranath. The latter considered him a close confidante and trusted him greatly. He frequently consulted him for everyday advice in the last two decades of his life. Prasanta and his wife, Nirmal Kumari, became his companions during the 1920s.

Their marriage was primarily opposed by *Rani's* father. But finally, seeing the sincerity of their devotion to each other, he gave his consent. Nirmal was the daughter of an educationalist, Heramba Chandra Maitra. Rabindranath fondly named her *Rani*.

Their marriage was solemnized according to Brahmo marriage rites by Satish Chandra Chakravarti. Rabindranath even attended their wedding and on the next day, presented the bound original manuscript of his musical opera, titled *Basanta*, as a wedding gift.

The bard blessed the couple and told them, 'As the premiere of the opera had taken place on your wedding day, the two of you alone have the right to this manuscript. I give this to you today!'

Rani Mahalanobis was a strong lady with a vibrant personality whose presence enriched the heart of Rabindranath during the early dawn of his life. Yes, the charming young lady became his beloved *Rani*, who, along with her husband, accompanied the ageing poet on his seafaring sojourns to Europe and to Southeast Asia for months. She seamlessly mingled into the household of Rabindranath and the bard, many years later, dedicated his poem 'Shyamoli' to her.

She was the last person, maybe the last woman, whom he was destined to tell, '*You are one of my last friends. I know that even if others go away, you will not leave me...*'

Years: 1927 onwards...

Nonetheless, Victoria Ocampo was like an inseparable shadow that refused to abandon his being, despite all the detachments between the two.

In the year 1927, Rabindranath began *Yogayog* and travelled across Southeast Asia. In the year 1928, he again went to England, hoping to give some lectures at Oxford. However, he had to return from Ceylon because of failing health and had to reschedule the plans of visiting Europe.

Maybe the bard was restless to seek another opportunity to ask Victoria to come to Europe. She—surrounded in a mysterious silence—was not even writing back to him.

In that silence, he suffered more and more, because there was none near him with whom he could share his hopes and his regrets.

In the year 1928, Rabindranath completed *Yogayog*, and he wrote the poetic novel *Shesher Kobita*. He even wrote most of the poems of *Mahua* during that time.

The poems of love and romance, in *Mahua,* were likely reminiscences of a memory which revolted against fading away and intensified his hopes to hear back from his Vijaya.

In *Shesher Kobita,* he perhaps lent Victoria's traits to Lavanya and some of her social characteristics to Katie Mitter. The backdrop of picturesque Shillong created a mystic aura of San Isidro, his own exploits at Villa Miralrío and Villa Ocampo.

The Last Meet: May 1930...

He met her again, in 1930, during his trip to Paris. Rabindranath had then matured into a full-bloomed visual artist, and he had brought a huge collection of his pictures with him in the hope of organizing an exhibition.

She took considerable pride and ecstasy in being able to arrange his first art exhibition at the *Galerie Pigalle.* The oval female face, with brooding eyes that came to haunt his art especially after that year, may well have a connection with her face. Only he, Rabindranath, knew it deep down. The exhibition was a success, was repeated in several other European cities, and was also taken to North America.

Alas, that was the last meeting between the Bard in Love and his muse, Victoria Ocampo. As the moment of parting arrived, inside the solitary hallway, Rabindranath held her fingers softly and said, 'Such soft fingers. I shall ever remain hungry for a touch of their tenderness. Do you remember these lines?'

Saying that, he whispered his poem, which he had perhaps written in San Isidro, while his voice reverberated across...

While walking on my solitary way
I met you at the dusk of nightfall
I was about to ask you to take my hand
When I gazed at your face, and was afraid.
For I saw there the glow of the fire that lay asleep
In the deep of your heart's dark silence…

Despite the strong bond, Victoria was never able to manage a visit to Santiniketan. The reason behind it remained buried within the hearts of the two, till eternity.

The play of dreams, Mayar Khela, generated a tornado within his failing mortal body while he kept on creating his masterpieces.

Amid the turmoil across the globe and his own traversal across various nations, Rabindranath felt the urgency of his own presence in Santiniketan to maintain the discipline and decorum of the institution of his dreams. He dedicated himself to protecting it and nurturing it so that it could become a timeless shrine of education.

As his age progressed, Rabindranath reflected upon the little Robi who still resided within the safe boundaries of his heart. In many of his works, he began to seek mercy from his most beloved Bouthakrun, who still denoted the epitome of love. It was a forgiveness for not being able to do something that could save her. It was forgiveness for becoming a global citizen and for being unable to remain the young man who only belonged to her with all his purity.

In 1937, he suffered from an episode of coma that

lasted for sixty hours. Yet, he was able to recover and continued his undeterred work.

Only, when he sat alone in his room, he laughed with a smile on his face and drops of tears near the brim of his eyes. '*Robi, my buddy... The time is arriving soon when we shall meet again and play together!*'

Shesher Kobita—The Last Poem

'Death is not extinguishing the light; it is only putting out the lamp because the dawn has come...'

Shesher Kobita is a famous work by Rabindranath. As the ailing poet remained in a déjà vu of his own life's journey, the world around him continued to bloom with the beauty of his creations. The meaning of love and despair metamorphosed into a sentiment of pure devotional and spiritual existence within his heart.

But, noticed by only a few, maybe the mischievous Robi was blossoming within him once more. Perhaps he wanted to play with his Bouthakrun and relive the moments like a carefree bird.

The years moved, and his mortal body aged. Yet, the heart of the bard remained in *love.* It was a love for creation. It was a love for life. It was a love for positivity. It was a love for memories. Spread across the decades, zigzagging through the years, the lives of many were touched by that beauty within his heart. Those episodes remained immortalized as pages of a beautiful album of reminiscences.

Brief episodes about his influences on the lives of prominent ladies marked the years. Yet, the relationships were more mature, and the towering personality of

Rabindranath left an impact on the lives of each and every person who had the opportunity of being in his company. In their hearts, he remained as a shining star for ages to come.

Among them, three names emerge within this tale of the bard, which have defined for him the meanings of three pillars during the dusk of his life… Songs, Sojourn and Strength.

Sahana Devi… Redefining the meaning of 'songs'…

Sahana Devi was born in the year 1897 into a family of stalwarts. Her distinguished family had a notable lineage of men and women on her paternal and maternal sides. Her paternal grandfather was Kali Narayan Gupta. He was a zamindar, a reformer and a lyricist who became a leader of the Brahmo Samaj. Her father, Dr Pyaree Mohan Gupta, was an acclaimed district civil surgeon. She was the beloved niece of Chittaranjan Das, the nationalist, freedom fighter and celebrated lawyer. Her mother, Tarala Devi, was his elder sister. Philanthropist, lawyer, composer, lyricist and singer Atul Prasad Sen was her cousin. Her maternal aunt, Amala Das, was a pioneer of Rabindra Sangeet and the first Indian woman to record songs in HMV. Despite the stellar familial background, the little girl was born to redefine her own destiny and create her own mark across the vast world.

Nonetheless, her life was like a ballad of tragedies that speckled the skyline ever since she was a child. Her father passed away when she was a little girl. Dr Pyaree Mohan had immense faith in his brother-in-law. Thus, as per his last wish, after his death, Tarala Devi and her children shifted to the South Calcutta residence of Chittaranjan Das.

Chittaranjan was a man whose heart was never devoid of love. Perhaps that is why the country fondly named him *Deshbandhu*, or 'Friend of the Nation'. He embraced them with all that he had, and Sahana started to grow up under his tutelage. Sahana followed him in his ideologies of open-mindedness, love, benevolence, independence, confidence, patriotism. Her inner strength was a reflection of him.

Sahana had a gift from God. Yes, a very special one too. She had the gift of *Songs*! It was a gift that was destined to be her identity.

She could memorize and perform any song effortlessly. Without even formal training, she was spontaneous in the art from a very early stage. At eight years of age, she heard the songs of *Lal Chand Boral* and could sing them with utmost perfection.

Chittaranjan once listened to her and said smilingly, 'Sahana, you must record your songs and name them… *An imitation of Boral*.'

Once, when Amala, her aunt, was teaching her sisters a *Toppa* song, little Sahana stood behind the curtain and listened to them quietly. Then, to everyone's surprise, she sang it seamlessly as they listened to her spellbound. The prodigious girl had learnt it on her own! With time, she could sing hundreds of songs altogether at a single go. Music was like oxygen, and she breathed it through the songs in her magical voice.

Rabindranath often frequented the residence of Chittaranjan. She first saw him in the house and felt that the man in front of her was serene like Jesus Christ. She was still a small girl and hardly did she knew how her life would become a part of the bard.

Sahana was first taken by Amala to sing in front of Rabindranath. The latter was at the residence of Chittaranjan, and Amala asked Sahana to sing something. While the little girl sat, closed her eyes and dived deep into the ocean of her gifted voice, Rabindranath became mesmerized. Thereafter, whenever he visited their residence, he summoned Sahana and listened to her. Unseen and unnoticed by any, a bond germinated between them.

At the age of fifteen, she sang at the *Magh-Utsav* of Jorashako. Concurrent to those years, she first visited Santiniketan to attend Rabindranath's birthday. That first experience of the serene quarters remained carved in her subconscious mind.

Formally, her Guru was Surendranath Banerjee of the Bishnupur Gharana, who trained her in music. However, she was far beyond any formal learning. She was a prodigy. Rabindranath sent Dinendranath Tagore as her teacher when she was twelve.

Atul Prasad Sen, whom Sahana fondly called *Bhai-Da*, taught her too. Once in Darjeeling, during a vacation, she was learning to sing from him. Rabindranath, coincidentally, was in Darjeeling too. One evening, Atul Prasad took her to visit the bard, and he listened to her songs in that vivid alpine environment.

As she finished, Rabindranath asked Atul Prasad humorously, 'What is the little music enthusiast saying currently? Is she singing nowadays?'

Atul Prasad beamed with pride and said, 'Her

affection is monumental. Even her enthusiasm is huge.'

Rabindranath looked at Sahana and replied, 'Enjoy, my child.... Women in this era either get married or get to sing! There is no middle path...'

Amid the passage of time, the jolts of destiny and the gift of music, Sahana metamorphosed into his beloved Jhunu in the heart of Rabindranath. Deep within, he knew she was special. He understood that she had something that no one did.

In the year 1916, she married Dr Vijay Bose. Alas, what followed was a tumultuous married life. But the little girl had matured into a strong woman by then. In the special bond she shared with the Rebellious Sun, Rabindranath became like a pillar for her. As she became deserted, she found her respite in the realms of music and songs.

She felt a special attachment, authority and love for Rabindranath and his songs. Once she told him, 'Gurudev, you are partial towards my singing...'

Rabindranath looked at her silently and then replied, 'Jhunu, you are saying this? What about your partiality towards my verses?'

Sahana was one of the only two singers allowed by Rabindranath to improvise his songs. In her voice and her gift of music, he could feel himself being reborn.

In the year 1926, she became terminally ill and sought permission by a letter to live in Santiniketan. Finally she arrived at the Abode of Peace, but for only a brief period of three months. However, those three months were like three decades that etched her presence in the world of Rabindranath.

One day, when she was a resident in Santiniketan,

he came into her room, measured her fever, sat in front of her quietly and looked at her face.

Softly he said, 'The experience that you have had seldom comes to the lives of people. There are so many restrictions and constraints. Thus, when opportunity comes, it breaks away everything and destroys all while going like a storm.'

She found strength in his voice and replied, 'That is what has happened to me. See, it came into my life like a tempest and blew away everything. It destroyed all and became my life. When my music found life in your songs, that tempest brewed and ultimately calmed down.'

His soft, caring and affectionate touch gave her a new life...

Soon, her illness turned into tuberculosis. In the year 1927, after those three months, she had to relocate to a sanatorium near Nainital. Rabindranath personally accompanied her till Kashi. From there, she went to Lucknow, to Atul Prasad's house. From Lucknow, her journey began into a solitary life at the sanatorium.

It took time, but she healed. But after healing, she never returned to the East. She traversed alone across southern India and finally went to Pondicherry. She spent the rest of her life at the ashram of Shri Aurobindo.

Rabindranath was very sad and heartbroken when Sahana Devi left. The *Gift of Songs* had created a divine bond between them.

When she went to the ashram at Pondicherry, he sent an unforgettable message: *'Whenever you sing my songs, I feel that my compositions have found their significance. Jhunu, in those songs, I am as much there as you are. It is for this subtle union that the composer in me awaits you!'*

Had I been an Emperor of ancient times, I would have sent my army to bring you back. My songs have the undying need for your voice...'

Moitreyi Devi... Redefining the meaning of 'Sojourn'...

Travel had always enriched Rabindranath's life. Ever since his first enlightening sojourn into the Himalayas with his Baba, he had sensed the importance of travel. Through happiness and sorrow, he had been a reluctant and an eager traveller simultaneously. It gave him companions and made him lonely, too. Across the country and in foreign lands, he had gained wisdom and pain.

And in that symphony, he truly became the Bard in Love...

Rabindranath visited and stayed at Mungpoo, a Himalayan hill station, a few times between the years 1938 and 1940. The sole inspiration behind the travels was someone who had carved a niche for herself as a noted Indian poet and novelist. She was Moitreyi Devi, and she played a vital role in taking care of the aged bard. In those final years, just like his last poems, love evolved as devotion towards a Guru from his pupils.

Moitreyi belonged to an aristocratic background. She was the daughter of Surendranath Dasgupta, the noted Indian scholar of Sanskrit and Indian philosophy. She was an educated woman who had a refined upbringing. She published her first book of poetry at sixteen, with a preface by Rabindranath himself. She was like a protégé of the bard.

Moitreyi had married Dr Manmohan Sen, a

quinologist who supervised the production of quinine from the bark of cinchona trees. He was posted at Mungpoo. Picturesque little Mungpoo had developed around a government-owned cinchona plantation ever since the previous century.

Rabindranath was fascinated by the bungalow at Mungpoo and had often mentioned it to Moitreyi in his letters. Once, he had written, '*You have such a mystic and beautiful bungalow amid the mountainous wilderness. Alas, the machinery of my own health is indisposed. So, it has become difficult to move around.*'

Moitreyi had a fascinating desire to host the illustrious poet in their bungalow, but was always sceptical about how well-equipped her abode was to take care of him. Then, one morning, a telegram arrived for her at Kalimpong. It read, '*Have just arrived. Will be pleased to see you.*'

Yes, Rabindranath was in Kalimpong, and he spent his birthday with them. That was the herald of a saga wherein the bard was to create some of his last few masterpieces.

In 1938 and 1939, she invited Rabindranath Tagore to stay in her and her husband's bungalow at Mungpoo near Kalimpong, which later became the *Rabindra Museum*. Her works include *Mongpoote Rabindranath* (translated later as 'Tagore by The Fire Side'), a record of his visit with her...

On the day he first arrived, the heavy showers were predominant...

It was as if the monsoons were welcoming his arrival. He had once cancelled the trip, but when Moitreyi sent him a basket of fruits at his home, Rabindranath told his son mischievously, 'I cannot delay my trip anymore. Moitreyi is angry and has thus started to send the delicacies of the feast to herself!'

At Mungpoo, Moitreyi and her husband had arranged for a chair and a few bearers to carry him upstairs into his designated room within the bungalow. Rabindranath came in and walked straight up the staircase. Midway, he turned back and said, 'Why do you worry so much? This place is like a palace to me!'

That evening, Rabindranath sat upon a chair beside the open window and looked outside at the settling mist. A few swallow birds had made a nest atop the bungalow and were busy chirping in the fading light of dusk. At a distance, a few lights were visible across the dark outline of the mammoth mountains.

He looked at Moitreyi and said, 'You win. You knew that this place would mesmerize me. That is why you were pressing so hard. They had said to me that they would first go and inspect the place, but I told them that I would see it myself. And then I shall know...'

As tears emerged across the brim of Moitreyi's eyes, he touched her head lovingly and said, 'See my dear. I have kept my word. I have come to you.'

The ravishing alpine beauty of Mungpoo used to create an ecstasy within Rabindranath. At his desk, there used to be a bell. One morning, everyone rushed in upon hearing its violent ringing.

As Moitreyi and the others arrived, Rabindranath handed over a letter and said, smilingly, 'I apologize for creating this commotion, but nobody was able to hear the bell for a long time. Here, Moitreyi, this is a letter that I have written to your father. Yesterday, I got a letter from him in which he had addressed me in poetry. Such acts often arouse the bard within me! If he, being a philosopher, can write to me in verses, then how can I, being a lifelong poet, stop myself and write back to him in prose? That is but impossible!'

As the sunlight used to fade beyond the horizon every evening, Rabindranath sat quietly in the darkness, lost in the depths of his own reminiscences. Perhaps the old and tired soul sought to look into the visions of his brilliant life.

In the comfortable, domestic atmosphere that centred around him, his literary musings blended with musical sessions and philosophical reflections that were richly strewed with fun, frolic and personal recollections of his early life. The quiet surroundings of Mungpoo might have helped to heighten a certain pleasure within him.

One evening, he sat down in a jovial mood and said, 'Let me tell you a story tonight. Many years ago, a proposal for marriage came to me from a distant province. The girl was the daughter of a rich zamindar and was heir to seven lakh rupees' worth of inheritance. Along with a few others, I went to meet their family. As we reached, I saw two young girls seated in front of us. One of them was average looking, sombre, quiet, and sat with a muted blank face. The other was jovial, pretty and smart. She was fluent in her English accent and even played the piano with sheer brilliance. My heart danced within my ribcage as she spoke chirpily about music and poetry. Then, the zamindar came and greeted us with his eloquence. He had aged gracefully and was courteous in his hospitality. After a while, he introduced the girls. He looked at the pretty girl and said, "Here is my wife!" Then he turned towards the sombre girl and said, "Here is my daughter! " That was a huge anticlimax. What do you think?'

He laughed and added, 'Well, after so many years, now I ponder...if I had consented to that marriage, then despite being a husband to a sombre wife, at least I could have inherited seven lakh rupees! That would have spared me so much of the hustle to save the financial health of Visva Bharati. On the contrary, I heard a rumour that the sombre girl got widowed soon after her marriage. Then, I thank myself for my decision, because it would have been truly difficult to save my own life had I been the husband!'

Rabindranath was twice present on his birthday at Mungpoo...

The first time, his hosts were anxious about how to observe this day. In Santiniketan, it would customarily be celebrated among a multitude of people. In Mungpoo, a remote and lonely village, it was impossible. Apparently, Rabindranath solved the problem on his own with a mischievous yet content smile.

He said thoughtfully, 'Why not invite the workers of the cinchona plantations and those at the nearby quinine factory, who form the native people of Mungpoo? I despise the gaping divide between workers and the so-called upper or middle class. Colonialism has planted such racial protocols about a babu and a worker. Why can they not celebrate together?'

He added, 'I refuse to abide by them. Since these people form the workforce and the lifeblood of Mungpoo, I wish to meet them on my birthday and celebrate it amongst them. Their smiles are more precious than anything else.'

Hence, the celebrations were completed in their midst as they recited, sang and danced in a tribal fete and offered him their respect.

On his eightieth birthday, the news of the death of his nephew, Surendranath, arrived. Rabindranath used to love him dearly. As the tears dried, he transformed the moments of grief by crafting a gem for his beloved nephew. He wrote a poem, dedicated to Surendranath, which was published in *Janmadiney* (poem #8). It was a book of poems that he had written on the occasion of his own eightieth birthday.

The sojourns at Mungpoo were witness to his innumerable memories. Moitreyi was witness to those prized moments that created fragments of the untold history of the Bard in Love.

Rabindranath believed what he stated, '*How are they, amid whom I have come? How are those people who pile the loads upon their horses and tread those treacherous terrains every day? I want to meet them. I want to know them...*'

He was a people's bard who always used to seek the company of people, the common people.

Indira Gandhi... Redefining the meaning of 'Strength'...

Indira Gandhi was born Indira Nehru, the daughter of Jawaharlal Nehru. Indira grew up with her mother, Kamala Nehru, at the family-owned estate, Anand Bhavan. Her father was often swept away in political activities, while her mother suffered from recurrent bouts of illness. She had limited contact with her father, and it was mostly through letters that she came closer to him. The separation first germinated into anger within the little girl. Then, it slowly mellowed and metamorphosed into a relationship of compassion and understanding.

Indira arrived in Santiniketan in the year 1934. With trepidation and confusion playing ruckus in her mind, she came to attend the school. During her interview, Rabindranath presented her with a name. He perhaps understood the turmoil that was brewing within the girl and had said, 'You are *Priyadarshini*...the one who looks at everything with kindness.'

Rabindranath was a stalwart and had an encompassing reputation, aura and magnificence that surrounded him. Indira felt shy and scared. The complete absence of teachers, classrooms or even formal students in the environment of Santiniketan fascinated her. The cultural shock was predominant, and a young Indira struggled initially to cope with the environment of the place. Age eroded a significant amount of patience from Rabindranath, and the latter remained visibly irritated and angry at times. Yet, soon the tides of time made the atmosphere conducive, and Indira found a fantastic teacher within him.

Indira had always seen a busy household. The political environment and the assemblage of numerous visitors never gave her a respite from being solitary. Moreover, there had never been much art or music in the space she had grown up. Being brought up in the politically sizzling familial surroundings, she was not prepared for the world of art and poetry.

Yet, in Santiniketan, Indira tasted the wild freedom of solitude. She drank the sweet nectar of music and even learnt dancing. Jawaharlal Nehru wanted his daughter to learn science. However, in her new abode, there was not much scope for that. So, he encouraged her to learn languages. Thus, Indira enrolled to take classes on Hindi, Bengali, French and German.

Despite every challenge, Indira Gandhi was a fighter. She fought her way into life and made her own prominent place in the heart of Rabindranath, who even commended her on her dancing abilities during a festival. For the first time, she was in a quiet place. She walked barefoot. She participated in early morning chants, rites centred around seasons, and even planted saplings.

The eyes of the bard, indeed, saw her as a pillar of strength. Once, he asked her, 'Indira, are you afraid of me?'

She replied hesitantly, 'No… I do not wish to disturb you.'

Maybe Rabindranath understood her dilemma, and that is why he persisted until she became a part of the small group who always accompanied him under the mahua tree while he painted or sang his songs.

Once, she had to return from Santiniketan to see her critically ill mother. Her father got released from jail and came too. However, Indira was heartbroken. As she went back to Santiniketan, she was as if afloat on a vast dark sea whose waves were trying to consume her.

Yet, Rabindranath and Santiniketan gradually became a refuge and a new world for her. It was in Santiniketan that she made new friends. It was there that she met Frank Oberdorf, a teacher who taught her French. He was deeply attracted to her and used to tell her, 'You are beautiful and unique...'

Indira became his friend despite the strong sentiments he had towards her. With him, she could share her happiness, sorrows, despairs, loneliness, anger and grief. Yes, it was in Santiniketan that she found a friend in whom she could unburden herself.

With Kamala Nehru's deteriorating health, Indira had to say her farewell to Santiniketan in the year 1935. Despite the brief association, Rabindranath and Indira Gandhi remained etched in each other's lives as personas of supreme strength. They complemented each other and enriched each other in a subtle way.

Rabindranath wrote to Jawaharlal Nehru with regret, '*It is with a heavy heart we bade farewell to Indira, for she was such an asset in our place. I have watched her very closely and felt admiration for the way you have brought her up.*'

The three pillars did get immortalized within the three ladies during the dusk of his life... *Songs, Sojourn and Strength.* They were vividly different from each other, yet they made a mark in his life just like he himself did in their own lives.

Time stops for none. So did the sand in the hourglass of his life run out...

Nonetheless, the Bard in Love created his ballads of romance and devotion in his memoirs. Similarly, his swansong too had a touch of the melancholy that remained like a shadow throughout his own life.

Rabindranath passed away on 7 August 1941. However, the legacy of his works remained a glowing epitome of his wonderful life.

Many episodes of his journey were erased, either to avoid controversy or to idolize him into a deity from a human being of flesh and blood.

Perhaps Rabindranath knew it. So, very cleverly, he had preserved his little Robi, the valiant Bhanusingha (or the Rebellious Sun), within his own songs, poems, and paintings!

In front lies the ocean of peace,
Launch the boat, Helmsman,
You will be the comrade forever...

Epilogue

To
Robi, my 'Inner Soul'

My dear friend, it has truly been a fantastic journey in this world as we have spent this life together! Thank you for telling this story to me while I have lived each moment.

The journey has been long, sometimes tiring yet exciting, but it is a journey that I have enjoyed to the fullest with you as my constant companion. Yes, you have kept your promise to be my BEST FRIEND forever, as our bizarre tale unfolded through your voice while we lived it together as inseparable entities.

From the first day in this world, to this very moment, I have experienced so much, met so many people, lost so many dear ones. However, as I stand at this hour of dusk, I can happily see the setting of the 'Rebellious Sun' beyond the never-ending horizon. Maybe this Golden Sunset would bring a new dawn tomorrow. Throughout this journey, I don't know whether I have become any wiser, but yes, I have tasted the touch of love, and that is the reason I have remained the unwise child who dreamt to do the impossible. From the very first day, the child in me had been a lone soul. Life gave me the touch of friendship and companionship at various points of this journey, but most of them had been momentary, just like the very essence of life itself. 'Love' is the purest of all emotions, and I am happy that I could cherish that gift. Yet, it follows the universal truth that nothing is perpetual. Only the sweet memories remain as an everlasting fragrance of those moments.

Yes, I was sceptical whether everything need's to be said or not, but today I do feel that everyone had to know about them and we had to echo them out to the world. Amid all, I am glad about the incredible feeling of being blessed with so much love. Perhaps, my poems and my verses would continue to safely harbour and protect those sentiments for ages to come. Yes, no scale can judge between virtue and vice. In this imperfect world, we too must remain imperfect within the harmony of our hearts.

Now, the sunset is about to be complete. Let us hold our hands and walk into the darkness so that we can together see the glittering opera of the starlit night. Tomorrow, the fresh morning will carry on the fragrance of our story.

Dear Robi, come with me, the time has arrived. As 'Best Friends', let us say our final goodbye in front of the entire human race.

Yours truly,
Rabindranath Tagore…your 'best friend'

Acknowledgements

Devoted to the Polymath who remains etched in our hearts as 'Gurudev'

Firstly, our deepest gratitude goes to our families, whose unwavering support has been fundamental to this work. Their encouragement and support have truly been the backbone of this work.

We are deeply grateful to the team at The Book Bakers, one of India's literary agencies, for their faith in this project. Thank you for guiding our literary path over the years and inspiring us to write this bold story about a stalwart of the world. Suhail Mathur, your unwavering support for this manuscript and all our works means a great deal to us. We truly value our bond with you and your entire team.

We deeply appreciate our dynamic publisher, Rupa Publications, for consistently supporting our work. We are also truly grateful to our devoted editor, Rudra Narayan Sharma from Rupa Publications, whose unwavering belief in this book has been invaluable. His personal dedication, expertise and trust in our vision have greatly enhanced this project. Thank you for your commitment to refining the manuscript to its finest version.

The Bard in Love is our heartfelt and honest endeavour to bring out glimpses from the life of an iconic man whose extraordinary creations have touched the lives of so many people in so many ways. His deep comprehension of human emotions, which evolved with his experiences with love, loss and life, has shaped his literary genius that continue to resonate with a global audience.